# BURN THAT PROJECT DOWN

A Salty Project Manager's Guide to Stand Out Without Burnout

---

KEN STEWART

Copyright © 2024 by Ken Stewart

All rights reserved.

No part of this book may be reproduced in any form or by any electronic or mechanical means, including information storage and retrieval systems, without written permission from the author, except for the use of brief quotations in a book review.

ISBN: 979-8-9911076-1-7

Interior Formatting by Sarah Symonds

# Contents

| | |
|---|---:|
| Acknowledgments | vii |
| Introduction | ix |
| 1. Building Your Signature System | 1 |
| 2. Get It Done; Be Decent About It | 9 |
| 3. Know the Game You're Playing | 17 |
| 4. You Are the Brand | 23 |
| 5. The Myth of the Perfect Plan | 31 |
| 6. The Illusion of Control | 37 |
| 7. Mastering the Small to Conquer the Big | 53 |
| 8. Beyond Words in Project Management | 59 |
| 9. The Dynamics of Herding Cats | 73 |
| 10. Building Bridges Between Dreamers and Realists | 83 |
| 11. Saving the Day Ruins the Team | 93 |
| 12. Scope Creep: The Monster Ate My Deadline | 101 |
| 13. The Whoosh and Thud of Deadlines | 111 |
| 14. Real Money Really Matters | 121 |
| 15. Chasing Quality: When Perfection Paralyzes Progress | 129 |
| 16. Flying in Uncertain Skies: Mastering Risk and Resilience | 135 |
| 17. Crisis Management: Duck, Cover, and What Comes Next | 147 |
| 18. Falling Victim to Fads and Gimmicks | 157 |
| 19. Embrace the Suck | 165 |
| 20. Escape Your Job's Emotional Shackles | 173 |
| Finale \| A Feast for the Vultures | 187 |
| About the Author | 191 |

## Dedication

*I would like to offer my humble dedication to the driving forces in my life.*

*Thank you, my God, for the ministry of writing. This process has renewed hope when I needed it the most and blessed me so that I may seek to bless others.*

*Melissa, my heartbeat, thank you for supporting me even as we walk through our darkest valley.*

*Mazey, our child of light, you continue to teach me lessons I never knew I needed to learn.*

*Finally, to you, my reader, live out your own purpose; it's your move!*

## Acknowledgments

Writing a book is never a solitary endeavor, and I am deeply grateful for the support and encouragement of several people who contributed to this project.

First and foremost, I would like to thank Melissa, who repeatedly told me to keep going and made this book possible. Your patience, understanding, and love have been invaluable.

I owe a special debt of gratitude to Raegen Pietrucha, my editor, for your insightful feedback, guidance, and encouragement throughout the writing process. Your acumen and expertise were instrumental in shaping this book.

To my friends and colleagues who volunteered to read my manuscript and provide feedback, Viraj Kasbekar, Cindy Zarnett, and Amber Cattin, thank you for your valuable input, inspiration, and for always being there to lend an ear or offer advice. Your camaraderie and support have meant the world to me.

A special thank-you to a friend and mentor who offered expert counsel during the development of this book. You asked not to be mentioned by name, but know that your heartfelt and humble guidance was truly appreciated.

Finally, I would like to extend my heartfelt gratitude to my readers. Your interest and support are what make this journey worthwhile. I hope this book provides you with salty insights and inspiration.

Thank you all for being a part of this journey.

Ken Stewart

## Introduction

### THE BITTER TRUTH ABOUT PROJECT MANAGEMENT

"The truth will set you free, but first it will piss you off."

—Gloria Steinem

Have you ever fantasized about your heroic, slow-motion walk away from the burning rubble of a project that just exploded in the backdrop of your life's movie? You're not alone.

If you're reading this, you may be facing down friction and frustration, disillusioned with what I call the "slog of war": a relentless battle against the daily grind of bureaucratic red tape, the monotonous drone of meetings better suited to emails, and the Herculean effort required to get so many people to agree with one another over minutiae that can seize projects faster than an ungreased motor. This relentless grind can lead to burnout, leaving even the most determined project leaders feeling defeated and deflated.

*Burn That Project Down* is a plain-language guide aimed at helping new and frustrated project managers—just like you—get high-friction projects done without losing your sanity in the process. I've watched so many project managers fall into the same trap time and again: They fail to be effective; miss avoidable communication opportunities; and, as a result, get lost, frustrated, and eventually just flame out. Their clueless foundering inflicts misery on everyone involved, and for some reason, everyone just accepts it as the only way to live. This guide offers direct lessons I've accumulated by falling and scraping my knees, bumping my head, bruising my ego, and eventually navigating to a successful outcome.

Here's the hard truth: Most project management advice is about as useful as a chocolate teapot. So why read any further? You don't need another guru selling you the latest, whiz-bang project tools or new-fangled frameworks. Forget those glossy books and overpriced bootcamps; they sell dreams, not reality. What you need is, well, practical advice. In the real world—where you and I live—your meticulously crafted burndown charts and risk assessments are as likely to hold up about as well as a house of cards in a tornado. When friction grows, you gotta get real to stand out without burning out.

Project management isn't for the faint-hearted or the hopelessly optimistic. Sure, it seems like an "Easy A" of a career at first, but it ain't. It's for the thick-skinned, the hard-nosed, the ones who don't flinch when the going gets tough. You're not managing a kindergarten, although you might feel like you are most of the time. You're running a project with deadlines tighter than a bank's security and a budget that's always two dimes short of a dollar. You gotta have grit.

It's time to get your projects out of the mud and back on the road. From initial battlefield conditions to pie-in-the-sky dreamers, this manual covers the practical bits about managing projects learned through decades of hard-won victories—and failures. If you're a new project manager, a frustrated project manager, or the boss of a project manager who is frustrating you, this book will give it to you straight.

Make no mistake about it: Books won't replace real-world experience. But it can help you avoid and navigate the challenges of your own project management journey. Guides like this can offer wisdom to help you navigate the challenges of your own project management journey, stand out as a go-to project leader, and most importantly build practical scaffolding to succeed without burning out.

Where do you start?

While starting at the beginning of the book makes the most sense to me, I've developed this book to be a kind of choose-your-own-adventure style reference. Yes, I've arranged the chapters in a certain order. That said, you are welcome to break the rules and read in any order you like. As you read on, I suggest you take what you want and leave the rest for the vultures' feast.

ONE

## Building Your Signature System

---

"Do not seek to follow in the footsteps of the wise; seek what they sought."

—Matsuo Basho

---

"Do you know the secret to being indispensable?" Sgt. Garner asked as we arrived at the Marine heavy helicopter squadron hangar to survey one of the outdated servers of Marine Aircraft Group 16. The two-year vacancy in our billets had left no staff to maintain the squadrons' messaging servers, and Sgt. Garner wasted no time in stepping into action once we were posted to the base.

"Follow orders?" I guessed.

We climbed the stairs to the top deck and made our way down the long hangar hallway to check in at S-1. As we signed the logbook, Gunnery Sgt. Hernandez called out, "Are you guys the computer techs?"

"Yes, Gunny," Sgt. Garner confirmed.

"The XO wants to see you," the gunny said robotically. "Take a left at the door; third door on your left."

Sgt. Garner and I exchanged a glance, and he shrugged before leading the way out the door. As Sgt. Garner made his way down the corridor, I noticed that each office had a small placard over the door. I read them as we walked: Commanding Officer, Sergeant Major, Executive Officer.

Sgt. Garner stepped into the open doorway and knocked on the heavy wooden door. "Gunny said you wanted to see us, sir?"

"Oh, the computer guys! We are glad to see you here," the XO said, relief spreading across his face. "We need to get stuff squared away for deployment; we're going on boat in a month. We've been having trouble with messaging for the past few days, and it's killing us. I don't know when the last time someone looked at the server was. Can you take care of us?"

"Absolutely, sir. We'll get you squared away." Sgt. Garner replied.

"Get with gunny on the details." And with a nod of his head, the XO returned his attention to some paperwork on his desk.

After getting our instructions from Gunny Hernandez, we set off to the server room to get the job done.

Our bootsteps echoed as we made our way across the red linoleum tiles. After a long walk, we arrived at a wooden closet door marked "Janitorial." Someone had placed a small strip of masking tape with the hand-scrawled word "Server" just under the official placard.

As we stood before the door, Sgt. Garner placed his hand on the knob and looked over his right shoulder. "Always be the bridge," he offered, answering the earlier question he'd posed to me.

"Bridge?" I repeated, unsure of his meaning. My gaze dropped to my boots as if the laces might hold the answer. Sgt. Garner squatted down in front of the old DEC server sitting on the dusty floor.

"That's the secret to being indispensable, Stewart. Bridges connect people from where they are to where they want to go. People always want a leader, but there's only ever one leader. Leaders, like the XO, can't do it all themselves. They need people who can translate and implement their vision into action that accomplishes the mission."

Sgt. Garner glanced up at me to confirm my understanding. "Always be the bridge, Stewart."

## It's Alive!

That moment is seared into my memory, and I vividly recall that conversation some three decades later. On that day, Sgt. Garner didn't waste time trying to prescribe any specific framework or give me step-by-step instructions to follow. Instead, he equipped me with the most vital perspective: how to think about being in the best position to succeed. Every tip, trick, and tool I learned from that point forward became part of a system I used to be the bridge; I've come to call this my signature system.

Your signature system is a Frankenstein-like creation of tried-and-true tips, tricks, and tools that you've figured out gets the job done. Whether you are a new project manager, a frustrated project manager, or the boss of a project manager who is frustrating you, a PM's got to find what works to get the job done.

Project management isn't just about fancy frameworks and debating the merits of Agile versus Waterfall methodologies. It's about experience, gut instinct, and the scars you earn from projects gone awry. While this guide isn't going to replace your real-world experience, it can help you fast-track developing your own way of doing the needful.

Crafting your own signature system is about taking what works, throwing out the nonsense, and making it your own. It's a lot like cooking. Sure, you start with a recipe, but the best cooks add a pinch of pepper, a dash of salt.

They taste; they adjust; they experiment. That's how you get a meal that's worth eating.

Here's the rub: Every PM's got their own palate. What works for one might be a disaster for another. So your system needs to be flexible. It's about understanding the principles, then adapting them to your style, your team, and your project.

## Taking Stock of Your Signature System

By this point, you might be struggling with what ingredients should be included in your own signature system. Here are the most common types of ingredients I've found during my time in the project kitchen:

**Your Tools:** These are the tools and templates you use to get the job done. They could be software tools like Microsoft Project or Atlassian Jira; templates like risk registers and charts; and even email and instant messaging software.

**Your Training:** Your education and learning must be relentless. Whether it's college courses for continuing education, new certifications, or books and podcasts, you must be diligent in your pursuit of lifelong learning.

**Your Process:** Your process is how you execute the work. You may follow your company's processes, bring your own frameworks, or mix and match what works best. Having repeatable, reliable methods to get the job done is a critical part of your signature system.

**Your Mindset:** Your mindset is perhaps the most important part of your signature system. Be intentionally curious, eternally adaptable, and develop unwavering grit.

**Your Network:** An often-missed aspect of a PM's signature system, building a network of supporters who help you get things done is critical to your long-term success.

As you turn these pages, keep this in mind: Not every tool, tactic, or tale will fit your palate. My goal is to help you with how to think about something rather than how to do it. So grab what works, and don't think twice about skipping what doesn't. This is about building your personalized playbook, not stuffing your bag with tools you'll never use. They'll be here collecting dust when you get to a spot where you realize you need them.

## Parting Embers

For now, what matters is building your signature system to be as unique as the person using it (i.e., you), filled with tools that are sharpened through use, not just shiny and new out of the box. And remember, the best PMs aren't born; they're forged in the fire of botched projects and impossible deadlines.

- **Be the Bridge:** Like Sgt. Garner advised, connect vision with action and lead by facilitating progress.

- **Create Your System:** Develop a unique approach combining proven tips, tricks, and tools tailored to your style and needs.
- **Adapt and Adjust:** Understand principles but personalize them; just like cooking, tweak and refine to suit your palate.
- **Experience Over Frameworks:** Value your experiences and instincts. Use this guide to fast-track your learning, not as a strict manual.
- **Flexibility Is Key:** Not every tool will fit every project. Focus on building a flexible system that evolves with you.
- **Learn From Mistakes:** Embrace the lessons from botched projects and tight deadlines; they forge the best PMs.

Remember, your signature system is unique to you. Sharpen your tools through use, and don't be afraid to discard what doesn't work. The journey to becoming an indispensable project manager starts with crafting a system that's distinctly yours.

Ready to roll up your sleeves? Let's get to work.

TWO

## Get It Done; Be Decent About It

"I've learned that people will forget what you said, people will forget what you did, but people will never forget how you made them feel."

—Maya Angelou

After a semester of exploring fictional suffering, Mrs. Jamison announced our next text: the Book of Job. "It's inspired many stories we've studied," she explained. Irritated but attempting to sound curious, I asked about the legality of studying a biblical text in school.

With a knowing smile, Mrs. Jamison reassured, "It's perfectly legal. We're examining it as literature, reflecting on its themes of endurance and faith, sanctioned by the school board."

I wasn't happy with the idea at all. I didn't like the idea of reading a book containing so many verses I had studied in Baptist Sunday School classes. The book seemed overly long, and I never could understand the point of a so-called "good god" who allowed his followers to suffer so much. But if I'm being honest, the real reason I didn't want to study this book was that I was wrestling with my own faith at the time.

I protested the assignment in and out of class. Finally, and determinedly, I confronted Mrs. Jamison. "I believe in the separation of church and state," I argued passionately. "Religion has no place in our school's curriculum."

Mrs. Jamison, accustomed to debate, proposed a compromise. "Clearly, this is a significant issue for you," she acknowledged. "How about an alternative approach? You still read the book, but instead of the standard analysis, you journal your critiques and frustrations. I'll review your entries weekly, offering feedback."

I considered her offer, weighing continued protest versus an open invitation to complain to someone who'd listen. Reluctantly, I agreed, seeing an opportunity to voice my concerns while fulfilling the curriculum requirements. Perhaps, if diligent enough in my rebuke, I could at least make the case for future generations to avoid this thinly veiled attempt at proselytization.

The assignment droned on. I turned in my writing journal week after week. Each week, I'd get comments back. There in the margins, with blue, green, orange, and purple ink, were her thoughts and observations about my entries. Mrs. Jamison was actually engaging with me and asking me questions, much to my surprise.

Somewhere along the way, I started looking forward to Mondays when I'd get my journal back. I looked forward to the questions and would get home and write new pages about what she had asked. I began to debate with her about the merits of her questions, to find there were more questions waiting.

As the final week arrived, Mrs. Jamison handed me my journal with a note in her cursive style: "I'm going to miss our interactions. Always challenge to understand. Keep your heart open to possibility." Her words lingered with me as the class buzzed around. I approached her desk to express my gratitude.

"Thank you, Mrs. Jamison, for challenging me at the start," I said.

"I enjoyed your challenges, too, Kenneth," she replied, smiling.

I left the classroom, the impact of our discussions echoing well beyond it. Mrs. Jamison had not only encouraged me to read Job but engaged me in a way that made me reconsider my views. This experience, though initially resisted, proved transformative, teaching me lessons beyond the curriculum.

## You're Graded on What You Get Done

As with any endeavor, it's important to understand how success is measured. So let's get one thing straight: Similar to school assignments you were once graded on, the only value you, as a project manager, add to the people signing your paycheck is the result—the successful delivery of the project. Of course, you'll forever be wrestling the iron triangle: budget, scope, and schedule. The mistake most project managers make is when they allow one of the aspects of the iron triangle to become an excuse for why the project is in the ditch.

Complaints and excuses come in a variety of shapes, sizes, and colors:

"Bob from accounting thinks he can squeeze blood from a stone with this budget cut."

"Looks like they've changed the scope again; might as well ask me to build a skyscraper with toothpicks!"

"The deadline's moved up? Sure, and I'll just hitch a ride on a unicorn to get it done on time."

Quit bellyaching! These types of passive-aggressive comments feel good in the moment but serve no purpose in achieving your goal.

Your job is to keep the project on the road or get it back on the road when it inevitably goes in the ditch. Truth be told, the people paying you don't give a rip about why the project founders. They grade you on your results—delivered or not.

Yes, you'll have to remind people that the increased scope will increase budget. Yes, you'll have to explain schedule delays. Yes, you'll have to play the tradeoff game with decision-makers. Just don't make the mistake that any of this is an excuse to allow a poorly performing project to persist. Projects always run off into the ditch. Your job isn't to make excuses; it's to keep them moving forward. Getting results is only half the battle.

## You're Remembered for How You Got It Done

Results put food on the table, but the way you get those results? That's the difference between a hearty pat on the back or a knife in the back when you least expect it. Yes, you get graded on the results you deliver. But that doesn't mean you should treat people like garbage along the way.

Sure, you could steamroll over everyone to get things done, but that's like using a sledgehammer to hang a picture on the wall; you're more likely to make a huge mess of things all the way around. People aren't disposable; they're the gears in a well-oiled machine that keep everything running smoothly. You treat them like garbage, and before you know it, you're the one getting taken out to the curb.

Being decent is being smart. These folks need you as much as they need a paycheck; treated poorly, the first time a better paycheck comes along, they'll be history.

Remember, word gets around. Treat your team like dirt, and that reputation will stick to you like mud.

In the end, how you get your results is your legacy. You want to be the project boss everyone respects, not the one they all moan about when you turn your back. It's simple: Do good work and treat people right. That's how you get remembered for the right reasons.

Reflecting on my experience with Mrs. Jamison, I realize she exemplified this principle perfectly. Instead of dismissing my objections to studying the Book of Job, she listened and offered a thoughtful compromise. Her approach not only defused my resistance but also engaged me in a meaningful way. She showed that handling challenges with respect and consideration can leave a lasting, positive impact.

Now that you've got the "why" of work, it's time to roll up your sleeves and shove your hands in the meaty mess of project management.

Remember, it's not just about getting things done; it's about how you get them done.

It's tempting to think the bridges you build or burn or the deadlines you meet or miss will be your legacy. But no; it's the choices you make that touch the people you meet along your journey. That is how you'll be remembered in the end. Mrs. Jamison's choices in how she handled my objections left a profound impression on me, teaching me that the manner in which you engage with others is as important as the outcomes you achieve.

## Parting Embers

As you navigate the often turbulent waters of project management, remember this: You're graded on your results but remembered for how you got them. Here are the key takeaways to keep your project on track and your reputation intact:

- **Deliver Results:** Your value lies in successful project delivery. No excuses; keep moving forward despite budget cuts, scope changes, and tight deadlines.
- **Avoid Excuses:** Don't let the iron triangle—budget, scope, and schedule—become an excuse. Address trade-offs and keep the project on track.
- **Respect Your Team:** Results matter, but so does how you achieve them. Treat your team with respect to build a positive reputation.
- **Build a Positive Legacy:** Your legacy is defined by your actions and interactions. Make it a positive one through smart choices regarding your behavior.

It's not just about getting things done; it's about how you get them done. That, in turn, defines your legacy. Do good work, treat people right, and you'll be remembered for the right reasons.

## THREE

## Know the Game You're Playing

> "War has rules, mud wrestling has rules—politics has no rules."
>
> —Ross Perot

I was at my wits' end! Despite my increasingly creative (and, let's be honest, less polite) refusals, the account managers just wouldn't back down. Here I was, a former customer turned evangelist, preaching the gospel of our revolutionary, service-led business model.

Imagine transitioning printer fleets from cumbersome, capitalized assets to sleek, no-hassle monthly subscriptions. In 2003, this was cutting-edge—a no-brainer today, but back then, it was like proposing a trip to Mars.

My goal was clear: help our sales team convince IT executives that this new model wasn't just viable but superior. Meanwhile, I was navigating a minefield of internal conflicts. The account managers, motivated purely by hitting revenue and unit targets, were all about the hard sell. Our shared goal was customer acquisition, but our methods? Not even in the same book, let alone on the same page.

The hardware, often sold at a loss, was just the bait. The real money lay in supplies and services—the seldom-considered cash cow quietly fueling our profit engine. However, my grand entrance coincided with the company's campaign to polish its sales force's tarnished reputation. No longer the "copier slugs" of old, our team was supposed to be sleek, savvy, and above board—though old habits die hard.

I introduced a suite of valuable add-ons, increasing our value proposition and potential profitability. The problem? Our sales team balked at the costs and risks. Each week brought the same old song: "There's no room in the deal," they'd argue. I was banging my head against the wall, trying to get them to understand that these add-ons weren't just expensive frills but essential components of our profitability.

Fed up, I sought refuge in a meeting with Toby, our company's owner. For 15 minutes, I vented my frustrations as he listened, nodding along. Finally, I exploded, "They won't take no for an answer, Toby!"

He smiled wryly and said, "If they took no for an answer, they wouldn't be very good salespeople, would they, Ken?"

That stopped me in my tracks. He was right. I was lost in a maze of my own making. Toby guided me through a reality check, which led to a pivotal question: "Have you considered aligning your model with their selling tactics?"

A bulb flickered on. These guys were masters at selling tangible widgets with fixed costs and clear risks. Here I was, pushing them into the murky waters of selling high-risk, intangible services. No wonder we were clashing.

Inspired by McDonald's, I revamped our offerings into "happy meals"—easy-to-digest packages with straightforward pricing and clear benefits. With management's support, we rolled out this new strategy to the sales team.

The result? A whopping 25% boost in profits in just a year, even as revenues climbed. Once we learned to play the right game, everything clicked—not just for us, but for our customers, too, who thrived working with a winning team.

## The Game Is Afoot!

Getting things done and being decent about it is just the ante to play the game. To stay alive, stay sane, and stay in the game, you need to know the rules of the game you're playing. Then—and only then—do you get to decide whether you're playing or not.

Most folks are clueless about the game they're playing—or worse, naively think they'll play the game by their rules. You gotta know the game and understand the rules.

What do I mean? If the people paying you measure you on getting results, then wouldn't it stand to reason you gotta know how to work within their system and get things done? Imagine going into a grocery store and trying to pay for your bread with a high-five; that ain't gonna fly.

Most places have a way they like to do things. Sometimes, they're written down. More often than not, you have to figure them out yourself (and in real-time). It's like tiptoeing through a minefield; one wrong step, and boom—there goes your leg.

Every project's got its politics, and politics is a game whose only rule is winning. Everyone's got an agenda, people have their quirks, and let's not forget that everyone is eyeballing how you do what you do and second-guessing how you should be doing it. Knowing the rules of the game—and playing it better than everyone else—gives you traction when things get muddy.

You also gotta know the players. Who's got your back? Who's going to throw you under the bus? How do you make friends, dodge enemies, and collaborate with frenemies? The rules only get you so far. Pay careful attention to the players in every project as well as those not directly involved who hold sway over the project (like a CEO or even a spouse). The cold, hard truth is that the measure of your success winds up being more perception than reality. What people think about you, your methods, and your track record more often comes down to your superior communication and positioning skills.

Once you know the game, its rules, and the players on the board, you get to decide whether you want to play. That decision is made every day, in every meeting you attend and in every email you send. Knowing the game I was playing allowed me to make hasty exits when I recognized major dysfunction early. Low integrity (e.g., lying or ethical violations), misrepresenting the job to be done, and blatant disrespect have been obvious reasons I've exited projects in my past; I don't cotton to the notion of hanging around when I see the writing on the wall. Yes, I've gritted my teeth and played the long game with some projects, too. Why? A couple of reasons: stacking up some hard-earned experience; padding the wallet; and, if I dare say it, a sense of duty—though now I wonder if it was more foolhardy than noble, truth be told.

Whether you stay or go, the important point to remember is that you are the one choosing. So don't be a passive-aggressive crybaby. Own your decision and be deliberate and unapologetic about it.

## Parting Embers

Understanding the game you're playing is what's important.

- **Know the Rules:** Recognize the written and unwritten rules where you work. Mastering these rules is crucial for navigating internal politics and achieving your goals.
- **Identify the Players:** Understand who supports you, who might oppose you, and how to collaborate effectively with everyone involved. This awareness helps you maneuver through the project's social landscape.
- **Adapt and Align:** Align your strategies with the existing system. Tailor your approach to fit the team's tactics, just as I did with our "happy meals" concept.
- **Make Informed Decisions:** Whether you choose to stay and fight or make a strategic exit, ensure your decision is informed, deliberate, and unapologetic. Own your choice and act with intention.

Being savvy about playing the game can make all the difference. Stay alert, stay flexible, and above all, don't jeopardize your integrity.

FOUR

## You Are the Brand

"A brand is the set of expectations, memories, stories, and relationships that, taken together, account for a consumer's decision to choose one product or service over another."

—Seth Godin

Corey, a straightforward entrepreneur with no time for niceties, dropped a bombshell during our project: "You need to start building your own personal brand."

Known for getting straight to the point, his advice was hard to ignore. From our days collaborating on a website rebrand, he knew I had a knack for writing and insights worth sharing. His advice was clear: Stop being the unseen hero and start positioning yourself as the product. This shift in perspective wasn't just a new way to work; it was a new way to live.

Your personal brand is more than a logo or catchy slogan; it's the promise you make to the world. It represents what you stand for—or what you want people to believe you stand for. Think of it as your professional handshake or your first impression. It's also your last line of defense.

Imagine your reputation as a tale told around a campfire in your absence. It's shaped by your actions and how consistently you perform over time, creating a lasting impression that can either open doors or close them—often before you even knock.

In the professional circus, your brand and reputation are not just add-ons; they are the very meat and potatoes of your career. While it might be comfortable to operate behind the scenes, today's project manager must see the value in a strong personal brand. It's not just about survival. It's about making proactive choices, leveraging both successes and failures to bolster your credibility and reliability.

A robust personal brand does more than allow you to appear effective; it enables you to be effective. Call it gravitas, chutzpah, or moxie, but whatever you call it, it grants you a degree of freedom that fuels a flywheel effect, propelling your career forward. As you become the go-to problem-solver, you transition from being a variable in the problem equation to a constant, dependable figure.

## Straight Talk on Personal Brand for the Salty PM

Even the saltiest of PMs can't afford to ignore the power of a solid personal brand. It ain't about slapping lipstick on a pig and calling it pretty. It's about trust, reliability, and the hard-earned respect that gets you through the project battlefield with your sanity—and your hide—intact.

Forget the fluff. Your personal brand is your word. It's what you're known for. Are you the PM who delivers on time, every time? Or are you the PM whose burndown chart is more slippery than a waterslide because you're always sliding your dates? Your personal brand is the difference between getting the nod when the next big project comes up or getting passed over in favor of the next guy.

So, yeah, while "brand" and "reputation" might sound like terms straight out of a marketer's playbook, they're as critical on the project battlefield as a clear charter and a solid team. Even the saltiest PMs need to manage them like the precious resources they are—or risk finding themselves sidelined, wondering where it all went wrong. Remember, in the end, it's not about the fluff; it's about getting the job done and surviving to battle another day.

## Fear and Loathing in Self-Promotion

In my experience, those who serve others have a natural disdain for self-promotion. I did, too, until my friend

Corey helped me recognize that by better positioning myself, I could not only work on projects I enjoyed but also help more people in the process.

It's not been a straight line of learning how to build my personal brand. There's a fine line between tending to one's personal brand and shamelessly pandering for attention.

One boss hit me over the head with, "I don't know how you get away with giving those Grammy acceptance speeches like you do, but somehow you come off as being authentic." It felt like a cheap sucker punch. After all, I was simply thanking those who supported me at the conclusion of a successful project. But it works for me because I am genuinely thankful for those people.

Another time, a boss pleasantly confided in me that she thought I was going to wash out after the first year because I was "too nice." You can be respectful and still get things done, come to find out.

My "North Star" directly aligns with my personal brand and has always guided me. I just needed to learn how to turn up the volume so more people could hear my story. It's confidence without being cocky. It's service without insufferable ego. It's results without the drama.

While we don't want to make a habit of generalizing, you and I likely have some shared experiences that create some hang-ups around self-promotion and personal branding. Stereotypes emerge for a reason.

Here are three common hang-ups you might be wrestling with:

**Welcome to the Ego Show:** So many treat their personal brand as a mirror. "Look at me!" they exclaim. If you are more focused on self than serving others, you'll wind up causing more damage than doing good. Healthy ego is knowing your worth, keeping your boundaries, and using your skills and talents to serve.

**Selling Is Selfish:** Selling can be self-focused or solution-focused. Top sales professionals understand that a sale should be about solving a key problem that provides a fair exchange of value. When you provide this fair exchange of value, it's OK to be proud of that.

**Asking for What I Want Is Selfish:** People can't read your mind. If you are a team player—ensuring the outcomes are achieved—there's nothing wrong with engaging with leadership, team members, and stakeholders to explain what you need to survive and thrive. Most of the time, if you've done a good job, others will want you to be successful in other endeavors.

Over the course of my personal and professional journey, I've come to recognize that most of my early hang-ups around self-promotion were related to poor self-image and weak personal boundaries. I felt like having any ego at all was inauthentic. I didn't want to inconvenience someone else by asking for support or an opportunity.

If you dismiss building your personal brand out of pocket by saying, "That's just not how I'm wired," I encourage you to consider some tactics I've adopted to help me build my own personal brand. You might find that building your personal brand is less about salesmanship and more about relationship—to you, to others, and to your future.

## Parting Embers

Your personal brand is not just an accessory; it's the very core of your professional existence. Here are the key takeaways to ensure you build and maintain a powerful personal brand:

- **Define Your Brand:** Who are you, and what do you want to be known for? While every detail may not be immediately clear, be sure you at least know "that one thing" that is most important to you.
- **Walk the Talk:** Say what you'll do and do what you'll say. A promise made should be a promise kept, or don't make it at all.
- **Be Consistently Excellent:** One-hit wonders don't build stellar reputations. Don't just talk a big game. Make sure you're backing it up with action, or you'll be branded a phony faster than you can spell "reputation."
- **Manage Mistakes Gracefully:** You're going to mess up. It's what you do next that counts. Make amends, learn, and move on.

Through authentic ownership and transparent learning, you can leverage mistakes to build back better than before.
- **Build Relationships:** Real connections beat a glammed-up social account of disengaged followers. People remember how you made them feel, not just what you did.
- **Evolve Strategically:** As you grow, so should your brand. But don't flip-flop on your core values. Be curious about how you fit into the landscape today and tomorrow. Ask, "What's next?" and, "How can I help with that?"
- **Ask for the Business:** As you master each of these, humbly and respectfully ask how you can engage with people you want to work with and projects you want to work on.

Your personal brand is the story others tell about you when you're not in the room. Make sure it's a tale of reliability, respect, and results. In the end, it's not just about the tasks you complete but how you conduct yourself along the way. Build your brand thoughtfully, and let it propel you toward greater success and fulfillment in your career.

FIVE

## The Myth of the Perfect Plan

"Everyone has a plan until they get punched in the mouth."

—Mike Tyson

I waited patiently before the attack, muscles coiled and ready to spring into action at my opponent's first twitch. I had it all planned out. Jim would throw a right hook. I'd step through and jam his right arm at the elbow with my left hand while shooting my yoked right hand up under his jaw just above his throat. With him now controlled, I could then step through and take him to the floor.

We faced. Jim leaned forward, beginning his first step to close the distance. I sprang into action. We both moved in toward each other to close distance as we'd trained for hundreds of times before. My left hand rose to block the impending right hook. My right elbow engaged, extending my right hand to find Jim's jawline. But just as quickly as it had started, I felt a sharp sting to my mouth as his right hand connected to my lower lip.

Instead of the expected hook, Jim slipped his right jab between my hands. I tasted metallic ooze and felt my lip already swelling. It had the intended effect, causing me to pause for a split second and reconsider my entire line of thinking. My training told me there was no time to worry; I had to keep moving.

As quickly as I registered the hit, I recognized my perfect plan was lost. It was time to let go and trust my training. "Just move!" I told myself.

I was still closing on Jim. Our bodies collided, and I imagined we looked like two kangaroos wrestling. My right hand connected with Jim's throat just below the jawline. My left hand—having missed its original target—quickly adjusted to palm the back of Jim's skull. With my left leg now behind Jim's right hip, I turned my own hips away from him, thrust my right hand forward toward the ceiling, and brought my left hand back toward my left hip.

Jim's head couldn't resist the counterpressures. It swiveled like a twist top from a bottle, and his body followed. Jim sprawled out perpendicularly on the mat in front of me, and I cocked my left arm for the final blow to his face.

Jim smiled at me: "Gotcha."

I stood up, shaking my head in disappointment, and offered Jim a hand up. "Yeah, that's what I deserve, fixating on my perfect plan. I forgot there isn't one."

## The Art of Expecting the Unexpected

You ever hear the joke about the project manager who made a perfect plan? The project manager is the punchline. Perfect plans are about as real as a unicorn in a tutu farting rainbows. In the gritty world of project management, the only certainty is uncertainty. Plans always change; if you can't stomach that, you're in for a world of hurt.

Now, don't get me wrong. I'm not saying planning and strategy are useless. But let's be clear: The battlefield of project management is littered with the carcasses of plans that couldn't survive first contact with reality. What they don't tell you in fancy courses is how to deal with Murphy's law: Anything that can go wrong will go wrong, usually at the worst possible time—simultaneously.

Plans are about as stable as a house of cards in a tornado. When you're planning a project, you're pretty much trying to predict the future. You think you've got all your ducks in a row, but here's the kicker: The world's got other ideas. You'll face unforeseen challenges, scope creep, resource shortages, and—if you're really lucky—a global crisis (or two).

Welcome to the real world, where change is the only constant.

But hey, don't go crying into your coffee just yet. This ain't necessarily a bad thing. Embracing change can be like reaching into the pocket of your old jacket and discovering a forgotten $20 tucked inside. It can lead to better ideas and more innovative solutions, and it might even open another door when things go south. The key is to be adaptable.

Expecting the unexpected is more art than science, I've found. Once you experience enough of it, you start to recognize the pattern is much like a Radiohead song metered in 10/4 timing—just on the edge of familiar but unnervingly elusive. Like a salty, weathered sailor, you know the storm's coming because you feel it in your bones. Experience has taught me to always have a Plan B. As a matter of fact, you might also want to have a Plan C, D, and E tucked in your back pocket.

Planning only gets you so far, though. The moment you think you've got it all figured out is the moment you get punched in the face. You can dodge and weave all you want, but feeling that first blow sets your mind reeling. Only the practiced PM doesn't get frazzled when hit in the face with real life. My advice is to toughen up and learn to take a punch.

Eventually, you'll learn to read the signs. Keeping your eye on the horizon, you'll start to notice dark clouds forming. When you see them, don't just stand around with a slack jaw. Act. That means constant monitoring, regular check-ins, and asking lots of questions.

Don't just prepare for risks; embrace them. Get to know them up close and personal. When you understand your risks, you control the game. Then risk can be a good thing. It becomes the soil where opportunity grows.

Remember, expecting a project plan to go smoothly is like expecting you'll win a fight blindfolded without the benefit of years of training. It's wishful thinking. The real skill lies in rolling with the punches, keeping important people in the loop, and coming out on top by managing expectations.

## Parting Embers

As you wade through your unpredictable world, remember it's not about sticking to the perfect plan; there isn't one. You must adapt when the plan goes haywire. Here are your key takeaways to stay agile and effective:

- **Flexibility Over Rigidity:** Expect plans to change. Stay flexible and adapt quickly when they do. The ability to pivot is crucial in navigating project chaos.
- **Embrace Uncertainty:** Recognize that uncertainty is a given. Develop contingency plans (B, C, D, and E) and be ready to choose an alternative if needed.

- **Learn to Take a Hit:** Just like in a fight, getting hit isn't the end; it's a call to action. Resilience and quick thinking are your best allies.

Planning is just the beginning. Your true test lies in how you manage the unexpected and turn potential setbacks into opportunities. It's not the punch that defines you but how you respond. Keep your team informed, always have a backup plan (or three), and stay adaptable.

SIX

## The Illusion of Control

---

"You like to claim that you're in charge of the world, but it's as if the world hasn't noticed and it does whatever it pleases in spite of you."

—Trish Mercer

---

"Hi, I'm Paul," the salt-and-pepper-haired stranger introduced himself. His button-down shirt and pocket protector perfectly pegged him as the Novell server migration expert I'd hired.

Novell had seen better days, and our latest client was ready to move into the modern era. In our initial meeting, I had suggested modernizing their tech stack, which would cut their monthly service costs by 20%. I closed the deal on a Tuesday and scheduled the upgrade for the following Saturday. With the clock ticking, I urgently needed a specialist.

I called Johnny, my recruiter at a national IT firm. "Hey, Johnny, I just sealed the deal with our client. We'll need that Novell expert next Saturday."

"Yep, we're all set," Johnny confirmed.

Come Saturday, as Mike, my network engineer, and I approached the client site, we were pleased to find Paul already there, his smile barely hiding his nerves.

"Well, let's get started," I said.

We made our way to the server room, greeted by a blast of dry, hot air—a reminder that our servers needed cooler climates to avoid damage.

Paul quickly took a seat at the console and began poking around. "This all seems fine," he nodded.

Mike then took over, switching to the newly configured Microsoft Exchange server. He initiated the migration. Everything appeared to be proceeding smoothly.

Stepping out onto the balcony, I leaned against the guardrail, a brief moment of pride washing over me.

"Uh, boss?" Mike's voice cut through my reverie.

I returned to find an "Unknown Failure" warning on the screen.

Mike and I exchanged a look and shrugged. "Hey, Paul?" I called, pointing at the message.

Paul took over at the console and started poking around. "I'm not sure what to do with this," he admitted.

"What do you mean?" I let the question float in the server room's hot air.

"Well, truth be told ... I've never actually migrated a Novell server to Exchange myself."

"But your CV ... " My words evaporated as I stood there, exasperated.

"I've managed Novell servers but never migrated one," Paul confessed.

"Well ... you aren't going to be much help, then, Paul. You should head on home," I said.

Mike and I faced the daunting task ourselves head-on, turning what was supposed to be a half-day job into a grueling 12-hour marathon we barely managed to complete. I thought I had thought of everything, until I realized I had overlooked the most obvious part: the people part, where life often has other ideas. The lesson was clear: Control is nothing but an illusion.

## The Conscious Competence Ladder

Everything is a power struggle until you realize it's not.

As a new PM, I thought my job was to control every aspect of the project. That meant it had to be under budget, on time, and of the highest quality. I thought I had to babysit all the personalities, and everyone had to get along. I thought I had to sell every decision or have the authority to make a tough call.

But the struggle I thought was outward just turned out to be a flawed perception of control. I didn't understand control is acquired through competence. And competence, as it turns out, is recognizing you will always be ignorant—at least about most things. That's a humbling thing to realize, but when you do, it sets you free.

You don't need some new-fangled framework; some frameworks stand the test of time. They can offer clever ways of understanding how to deal with the messy problems people bring with them.

One such framework I've found invaluable is The Conscious Competent Ladder. Back in the '70s, Noel Burch cooked up novel way of thinking about skills. While I'd debate whether it's more of a circle than a straight, up-or-down ladder, the concept is rock-solid. Whatever way you wind up thinking about it, there are four distinct phases.

Most of us start off as unconscious incompetents, blissfully unaware of a complete lack of skill or knowledge about a specific topic. Unfortunately, at this stage, people's confidence often far exceeds their skill. Experience shows that unconscious incompetents find it hard to judge just how unskilled they really are, which you might know as the Dunning-Kruger effect.

In my experience, these folks can be the most hazardous to deal with as leaders or customers. Out of seemingly nowhere, you may find yourself with a customer, a boss, or some other influential person that, woefully self-unaware, is creating lots of friction for you. It's useful, in such moments, to recognize the difference in motivations between the unconscious incompetent and an actively engaged dissident. The active dissident is trying to deep-six you, the project, or both, while the unconscious incompetent naively thinks they know better and wants to help. The unconscious incompetent generally agrees on the goal but may argue with your method and dole out advice like candy to kids at Halloween, the difference being that the kids actually want that candy. You've gotta be assertive, set your boundaries, and on rare occasions put 'em in a joint lock—metaphorically, of course.

At some point, something clicks, and the unconscious incompetent sobers up. The newly conscious incompetent is hit in the face with the cold, hard truth and realizes just how ill-prepared they are. As project managers, this is where most folks throw in the towel and give up. A few brave, high-caliber PMs will saddle up for the long ride. Coachable and eager to learn, the conscious incompetent who leans into adversity is ready to develop grit and achieve success.

Eventually, conscious incompetents finally get the hang of things, but much like driving a stick shift for the first time, they're fumbling and in need of constant attention. Every so often, they might get a glimpse of what it feels like to truly master the skill, but the effort still requires a lot of focus and might make you feel like downing a stiff drink by the end of the week.

The unconscious competent finally emerges. They've got this thing down pat, like cookin' eggs and bacon on a Saturday morning. And just when they think they know everything about a thing, the truly gritty PMs realize there's a whole ocean of stuff they don't know. And so the cycle starts all over again, a never-ending carnival ride.

## How to Climb the Ladder

Theory is nice, but how is all this jabbering gonna help you? Here's the meat and potatoes:

**Handle the Unconscious Incompetents:** You'll meet plenty of these know-nothings. Handle them with care. Assert yourself, but remember, they probably think they're helping. Educate them if you can, tolerate them if you must, but don't let them derail the train in either case.

**Guide the Conscious Incompetents:** These folks have just realized they're out of their depth. Be a mentor, not a tormentor. Encourage their learning and give them food to grow. Remember, your path started here, too.

**Support the Conscious Competents:** These folks are getting the hang of things but aren't quite there yet. They're like kids learning to ride a bike. Be patient, provide guidance, and let them wobble a bit. If you are the conscious competent, be sure to ask for the same.

**Learn From the Unconscious Competents:** On the off chance you get to work with one, pay attention; watch and learn from them. Most are like mysterious kung fu masters who rarely reveal their secrets. Ask a lot of questions, and when they do give you a rare glimpse at their playbook, pay attention.

**Recognize Your Ignorance:** You don't know everything, and that's okay. Admitting your ignorance is the first step to actually learning something worthwhile. Stop pretending and start listening.

**Drop the Illusion of Control:** Eventually, you'll figure it out. You are not the puppet master of your projects. Things will go sideways no matter how tight you grip the reins. Learn to adapt instead of trying to control every little thing.

In the end, high-caliber PMs recognize control ain't about holding on; it's knowing when to let go.

## What You Can Control

Controlling a project is like attempting to hold onto a greased pig: It's slippery, messy, and you're probably gonna make a fool of yourself trying. But like any grizzled project manager, you've got to learn the difference between what you can wrangle and what's just going to slip out of your grip and make a fool of you anyway. There are a few things you can influence:

**Your Actions:** The most obvious thing you can influence are your own actions and decisions. You don't have unlimited resources or time, and you likely have only a handful of practical choices in any given situation. The important point is that you still get to make the choice and decide your next step.

Well, if it's so obvious, why am I having to say it? Because after all these years, I'm still shocked at how often I have to remind folks of the fact that they have choices in every situation. Reflecting on your options in every situation is one of your nonnegotiable habits. Practice often.

Oh, and keep in mind, every decision you make is like dropping a pebble in a pond. There are ripples. Don't just decide and act; anticipate the effects of your decision.

**Your Communications:** I've said it already, but let me say it again: How you frame things is an often-missed secret to chalking up W's and avoiding L's. How you convey information to your team, bosses, stakeholders, and even that guy who keeps stealing your lunch from the fridge is on you. Clear, concise, and no-nonsense communication can save a lot of headaches in the end.

**Your Signature System:** Being successful in any given project is all about how well your signature system is built and how well you follow it. What is your signature system, you ask? It's how you do what you do to get results the way you want.

Your signature system is your tried-and-true method to dance with and dominate insanity. Whether or not you've already got all the tools, frameworks, and strategies you need, what's going to set you apart is your system for getting things done. The company, the customer, and other people may all have their way of doing things. Your system has to be simple and flexible enough to accommodate insanity without going insane yourself.

## What You Can't Control

There are more than a few things you can't control. It doesn't mean there aren't ways to deal with them, though. Let's look at the key things you'll have to wrestle with as a PM:

**Other People's Actions (and Emotions):** You're not a puppet master. Folks will do what they will, sometimes screwing up (or screwing you) royally. You can guide, advise, and rant all you want, but at the end of the day, they're their own person. They make choices, and you have to decide what to do with that.

Likewise, you can't control others' emotions. You'll get all manner of behaviors, and when (not if) you come face to face with the darker side of team dynamics, you'd best deal with it and not dawdle. Stay curious, check your ego, don't get baited, and hold firm to your boundaries. Remember, you can control your actions and decisions. That's how you influence the outcome in situations where things get messy. When the greased pig gets away from you, don't dive to catch it. Just close the gate.

**Your Environment:** Unless you've got a crystal ball, you can't predict market shifts, global pandemics, or if the coffee machine will break down on the day of a big presentation. Whether we're talking about economics, sales, or company politics, you can't control your environment. The best you can do is decide whether to stay or go. If you are going to stay, take off the rose-colored glasses and pay close attention to reality. Then act accordingly (emphasis on "act").

**Past Decisions:** What's done is done. If you or someone else made a blunder, recognize it, learn from it, and move on. Droning on about the past is about as useless as closing the gate after the pig got loose. You'd best be thinking about how to get the pig back in the pen before your bacon up and leaves for good.

## Choking Progress: The Art of Micromanaging

Micromanaging is the art of annoying everyone around you while simultaneously choking your project to death with your bare hands. The brutal truth is that micromanaging is a clear sign that you're insecure and need to grow up. Micromanagement is an illusion of control that tempts you into thinking you are pulling all the strings. However, it doesn't scale, and worse, you cut your teammates' legs out from beneath them in the process.

While you think you are trying to help, you're really smothering the project. When you micromanage, you're telling your team you don't trust them to tie their own shoelaces. It's like giving everyone a playbook on how to hate coming to work. You'll see creativity and motivation disappear—swiftly.

And productivity? Forget about it. You're creating more bottlenecks than a traffic jam in New York City. Your team will spend more time chasing every microscopic detail than actually doing the work.

If you have an ounce of sense, you'll step back, delegate like a pro, and watch your team do what they do best. If not, here's what's in store for you:

**Killing Your Team's Morale:** If you don't trust your team to do their jobs, they'll start doubting themselves. Soon enough, they'll have less drive than a parked car with a flat tire.

**Stifling Your Team's Creativity:** You hired these people for a reason, right? Let them show you what they've got. If you're always dictating how things should be done, you'll never see the full potential of your team's creativity.

**Losing Sight of the Bigger Picture:** While you're busy nitpicking font sizes in a presentation, you might miss a looming deadline or a critical flaw in your project plan. Micromanaging is like looking at rear view mirrors: Everything seems smaller and farther away.

**Exhaustion (for Everyone Involved):** You're not a machine, and neither is your team. Trying to control every little aspect of a project is like honking at every car that passes—futile and frustrating.

Remember that project management isn't about controlling everything. It's about steering the vehicle in the right direction, knowing when to adjust the speed and when to let the crew take the wheel. Control what you can, influence where you can, and for the love of sanity, let go of the illusion that you can control everything.

## Let Go of Your Inner Micromanager

Do you have a tendency to micromanage? How should you step back, scale your system, and still deliver results? Even after years of practice, I find I have to occasionally remind myself to retrench my position. Here's some no-nonsense advice I've learned in my years:

**Recognize Anxiety:** I found that a lot of my desire to micromanage stemmed from anxiety around failure or letting people down. When I recognized my emotions creeping up, I learned to get curious about what they are telling me. Then I can consciously apply my problem-solving tactics.

**Focus on the Big Picture:** Think about your destination instead of tripping over every stone on the road. Understand your project goals, align with your team on the details, and trust them to come up with how you'll get there.

**Delegate:** Start with something small, hand it over to a team member, and set clear expectations. Let them handle it.

**Schedule Follow-Ups:** Instead of hovering like a helicopter, set up regular check-ins. Only peek in the PM oven at set times when you're baking the cake. If you trust the process, you and your team will bake a beautiful cake together.

**Ask Questions:** When you do check in, ask questions. Don't nitpick. Encourage and guide, don't scold, and ask things that genuinely reflect curiosity and are designed to help you get specific items on track and planned sufficiently.

**Trust, but Verify:** Trust your team and keep an eye on the progress. This is a great chance to ask more questions. Eventually, your team will learn to anticipate them before you ask.

**Be Consistent:** I can't emphasize this enough. Your team should easily be able to figure out what to expect from you and you from them. This accelerates psychological safety and encourages your team to move up the Conscious Competent Ladder. When you aren't consistent, an anti-pattern forms—one that has more negative consequences than positive ones. Your team learns they can't trust you, and that's when you lose.

Rome wasn't built in a day, and neither is breaking the habit of micromanagement. It's gonna take some time, patience, a lot of biting your tongue, and maybe even some therapy. But stick with it, and maybe, just maybe, your team won't be plotting your disappearance.

## Parting Embers

Control is more about adaptability than rigidity. Here are the key takeaways to help you thrive amidst chaos:

- **Acknowledge What You Can't Control:** You can't control other people's actions, the environment, or past decisions. Recognize these limitations and adapt your strategies accordingly.
- **Focus on What You Can Control:** Your actions, decisions, and communications are within your control. Make thoughtful choices, communicate clearly, and consistently follow your signature system.
- **Let Go of Your Inner Micromanager:** Resist the urge to micromanage. Delegate responsibilities, trust your team, and provide guidance instead of trying to control every detail.
- **Embrace the Cycle of Conscious Competency:** Recognize that mastery is a continuous process. Move through the stages of competence with humility and a willingness to learn, knowing that each phase brings new challenges and insights.

Ultimately, project management isn't about controlling every detail but about steering the project with wisdom and flexibility. Let go of the illusion of control, empower your team, and focus on what truly matters: delivering results through collaboration and trust.

SEVEN

# Mastering the Small to Conquer the Big

---

"He who is faithful in a very little thing is also faithful in much; and he who is dishonest in a very little thing is also dishonest in much."

—Luke 16:10 (Amplified Bible)

---

"Girl, you need to *dump! That! Man!*" Anna told the customer on the other end of the phone, the last three words thumping like distinct beats on a drum. "He is no good for you!"

"What did I walk into?" I thought as I approached.

Anna hung up the phone some minutes later, at which point, I asked, "Who was that?"

"Oh, that was Janice," Anna offered, as if that was all I needed to know.

"And what did she need help with?"

"Oh, she couldn't get her Word application to print."

I nodded. "Well, did you get that fixed?"

"Hmm?" she said with a furl of her brows. Then it clicked. "Oh, no. I told her she needed to get with her IT group for that."

Given that was the case, I asked a follow-up question: "So what was the rest of that about?"

Anna cocked her head and let loose. "Let me tell you, she has a deadbeat boyfriend that doesn't want to work and doesn't take care of anything around the house! So I told her she needs to recognize she is a queen and deserves better."

Moments later, I got a call from the front desk informing me that a customer was on the line and wanted to talk about Anna.

"Did you happen to get a name?" I asked our receptionist.

"Janice," the receptionist's voice offered.

I shook my head and prepared myself for a diatribe about how Anna didn't solve the customer's problem and instead exacerbated another one. As I picked up the phone and braced for the incoming salvo of angry vitriol, my fears lifted like smoke when Janice explained to me, in no uncertain terms, that whatever we were paying Anna wasn't enough.

## Care About the Details

Anna's reputation grew from her ability to manage people and projects with equal care. Her candid advice to Janice shifted the focus to what mattered most to Janice and reflected her genuine concern for Janice as a person. This small act of kindness made a big impact in Janice's life and became a hallmark of Anna's career. Her attentiveness to minor details, whether technical or personal, showcased her faithfulness in little things, encouraging other leaders to place increasing trust in her.

As Anna transitioned from customer support roles into project leadership positions, her reputation became synonymous with style and solutions. Leaders trusted her not only for her ability to manage projects through to resolution but also for her panache in doing so.

Anna genuinely cared for people as much as for the projects she fostered. Her teams depended on her for advice on getting the job done and feeling good about it along the way. Customers returned time and again, citing the reason they stayed with the companies she worked for as her caring approach to their concerns.

When you understand how to align yourself with what matters most to your team and your stakeholders, others take notice that you notice them. Their details matter, and if you are genuine in your concern for what matters to them, many will reciprocate with opportunities you might not yet imagine.

## From Small Acts Grows Great Trust

Paying attention to the little things matters. It's the small acts of diligence and care that build the foundation for larger responsibilities. Anna's journey from handling customer support calls to leading projects exemplifies this principle. Her ability to manage minor issues with genuine concern and precision earned her the trust and respect of her peers and leaders alike.

What might seem like minutiae to those who aren't wired like Anna often holds significant importance. It's easy to dismiss advice about focusing on details as tedious until you face a critical problem that hinges on one of those small yet material details. Remember how Anna's attention to Janice's personal troubles, while seemingly unrelated to her technical issue, created a strong bond and trust? This is a prime example of how small, seemingly insignificant actions can lead to significant outcomes. When we address the little things faithfully, we prepare ourselves for larger challenges.

When you listen to guidance, ask questions to understand, and mind the details during execution, you build trust. That trust leads to more trust and more grace when things get missed. Much like a length of string being wound, this ball of trust starts small and grows over time.

This is how we grow—by learning details and demonstrating trust. While Anna had a natural predisposition for this, I've had to learn these lessons a harder way.

Through years of training in the military and in martial arts, I learned we execute to our training. As a goal-oriented project manager, I had to learn to mind and master details. Eventually, it became clear that when we fail to master the details, we fail to master the outcome. We become experts at our craft by mastering the small to conquer the big.

## Parting Embers

Mastering the small details lays the foundation for conquering the big challenges. Here are the key takeaways to ensure you're not just getting things done but doing them right:

- **Concern Yourself With Others' Concerns:** When you genuinely care about what matters to others, you build meaningful relationships and trust.
- **It's the Little Things:** Handling small tasks with care and attention also builds the trust needed for assuming bigger responsibilities. Master the details to earn and keep the trust of your team and customers—and to scale up.

It's the small, seemingly insignificant actions that often lead to significant outcomes. Your attention to detail, timely actions, and reliability define your reputation as a project manager. Master the details, demonstrate why you can be trusted, and you'll be trusted with increasing responsibility.

EIGHT

# Beyond Words in Project Management

"The most important thing in communication is to hear what isn't being said."

—Peter Drucker

Troy kept pulling me off balance. "You keep giving me all this tension," his assessment echoed in my head as I faced all 6 feet, 4 inches of him. Our hands vied for control in the space between us during the classic kung fu drill, chi sao. Every time I adjusted my hands, Troy would feint, causing my arms to twist awkwardly. Thwack! The first punch landed on my chest, quickly followed by two more. Thwack, thwack!

Our hands tangled again, twisting in a blur. Suddenly, my right cheek was pressed against Troy's chest as he unbalanced me once more. Our sifu chuckled heartily from the sidelines, watching me struggle and growl in frustration with each failed attempt to remain upright.

"Ken, you are giving me all this tension and stress," Troy repeated. He looked down at my left hand to make his point. My attention instinctively followed.

"I know—relax harder," I sighed, my gaze dropping to the floor with the weight of my frustration.

Our wrists met once again, and the dance resumed. This time, I noticed a slight tension in my left hand as Troy attempted to pull me off balance me. I let my left elbow fully relax, and Troy's grip slipped, leaving my hand behind. I had caught the subtle tension in Troy's right arm, which would normally prompt me to tense up in anticipation of a struggle. Instead of resisting, I relaxed and found my balance, ready for his next move.

Troy paused, a knowing smile spreading across his face.

"Relax harder!" I said with a newfound confidence.

"Now you understand," Troy said. "When you stop resisting and relax, your senses open up—not just to what you see and hear, but to everything."

What an apt lesson for life and especially for effective communication. Often, we need to listen for what isn't explicitly said and learn to communicate above all noise. Through my career, I've integrated a handful of high-impact tactics into my signature system, which has significantly improved how I manage projects and lead teams. Let's get into them.

## Steer the Narrative

As the captain of your ship, how you steer through storms is one of the key skills in surviving as a project manager. Much like in chi sao, where maintaining balance amidst feints and shifts is crucial, navigating project management requires similar poise. Even if you're off track and over budget, you can still tell your story the way it needs tellin'. And it's not all smoke and mirrors. Every PM worth their salt knows how to steer the narrative so people keep their facts straight in the midst of the squall.

Did you clash with a stakeholder, much like a sudden feint in chi sao? Face a missed milestone, feeling the pressure building? Act quickly. Loop in your chain of command. Frame your story clearly so others see the truth.

The things you say (or don't) or write (or don't) are the often-missed, secret ingredient that makes the difference in whether your story is remembered as a masterpiece or a mess in the minds of those who matter most. Effective communication to your team, bosses, and stakeholders is more about ensuring the real story is understood rather than merely delivering the project on time or under budget. Just as I learned to perceive subtle tensions during training, seasoned professionals must guide the narrative to avoid becoming the subject of rumors.

Steering the narrative is about responsibly managing the perception of progress. While you and I know control is an illusion—much like the dance of chi sao, where true balance is dynamic—most folks prefer to live in the Matrix because it's that very illusion that makes them feel like it's all going to be OK.

It's your job, as the PM, to have a plan for every outcome and communicate how you see it getting done. Is it possible to have a plan for everything? Perhaps not, but top-performing PMs sure make it seem that way by staying attuned to spoken and unspoken signals, just like sensing your opponent's next move.

## Frame Your Plan, Flex the Details

I figured out early on that I am not smart enough to anticipate every little detail of a project. Instead, I learned to create basic scaffolds for my plans, allowing the details to flex as the situation developed, much like in chi sao, where you must adapt to your partner's movements. You can typically expect a few general outcomes in any scenario: Folks agree, they disagree, they won't commit, or they ghost you.

**They Agree:** When they agree with you, you'd best not stand around slack-jawed. Just as I had to be ready for Troy's next move, you should have your team picked out, know the basic resources you'll need, qualify your risks, and align on a snapshot timeline.

**They Disagree:** This is the scenario everyone frets over. They wind up getting flustered and frantic. According to Rick Maurer, there are 3 levels of resistance: They don't get it (and need more information), they don't like it, or they don't like you. Heck, it might be any combination or all three, in fact. Figure this magic combination out, and you'll know how to get the agreement you're looking for, or at least when to cut bait.

This isn't about manipulation; you have to understand the root of disagreement. Is it a lack of information, a fundamental difference in perspective, or something else entirely? Address these concerns directly and respectfully. Try to find common ground or a compromise. This is wisdom—understanding that disagreement isn't an obstacle to overcome by any means necessary, but an opportunity for dialogue and alignment, much like sensing and responding to subtle cues in chi sao.

**They Won't Commit:** I'll never forget the lesson I learned when negotiating with some Japanese clients. I mistook polite acknowledgment for agreement, which stalled the project. After a few weeks, my boss explained that "Hai" didn't mean "Yes" like I thought it did. It simply meant they politely acknowledged I said words. Aside from my glaring lack of linguistic acumen, I learned to treat noncommitment just like disagreement. Understanding the unspoken nuances is crucial, much like interpreting Troy's subtle shifts.

**They Ghost You:** Sadly, this scenario happens all too often. People are overworked and self-interested. When they don't see a need to provide any feedback or acknowledge your effort, it simply means you're less important than something else that has their focus. Dealing with this is pretty straightforward.

If you don't need their input, move along. If you do need their agreement, you've got a few choices:

**Check In With Your Main Contact:** Directly handle the situation with the person using various communications tools (i.e., emails, IMs, meetings). The most likely reason for radio silence is that they are underwater with day-to-day stuff. At some point in my follow-ups, I deploy the phrase "as a professional courtesy." It may read a little something like this, "I understand you are busy. As a professional courtesy, I would really appreciate your response to move this forward."

**Aim Above Them:** If Option 1 fails, start climbing their chain of command until you get an answer (and inform your boss that's what you're doing).

**Prepare for Detonation:** If Options 1 and 2 don't work, let your boss know the project is blocked and prepare for things to blow up. Sometimes, you need other, more influential people to apply some pressure. Just as a well-timed frag grenade on the battlefield gets attention, persistence and escalating the issue can make a difference.

## Manage Your Trust Bank

Trust is a currency. You earn it, save it, and spend it. Relationships run on this currency. Earning trust is like making deposits into an invisible bank account. With a balance, you spend trust as needed; without it, you face a deficit that quickly accumulates interest.

Just as I had to learn to trust in the process of kung fu training and my chi sao partner, Troy, trust in project management must be carefully cultivated and maintained with practiced repetition.

Relationships are built for mutual benefit, and the amount of trust required to achieve a desired goal matters. Being assertive, curious, decisive, and direct are the hallmarks of my communication style. Along with my ability to deliver results, my style allows me to easily build trust and make regular deposits in my trust bank. Your style may be different, and you have to learn how to use it equally well to increase the balance in your trust bank.

Stakeholders need assurance that their trust is well-placed with you. Your capacity to guide the narrative directly correlates with how effectively you manage your trust bank. If it's been well-tended, your narrative will be more believable, and you can make withdrawals to help support your narrative. If you make too many withdrawals, you will become overdrawn, and your stakeholders will no longer see you as a trustworthy partner, eventually closing their accounts.

Keep in mind, growing your balance takes time. Just as mastering the subtleties of kung fu requires patient practice, you must successfully deliver results, build mutually beneficial relationships, and ensure you are always being of service to those signing your check. As your balance grows, so too will your influence over the narrative.

## Say It Already

Too often, project managers hesitate to speak up. On a call with a supervisor, I noticed his discomfort—squirming as if on a hook, his body language betraying his stress over a particular idea. I could've said nothing. I could've been more delicate. Instead, I just said it: "Boss, you look more twisted up than a pretzel. Let me analyze the data, and I'll have a revised plan for you by tomorrow. How does that sound?" Everyone erupted in relieved laughter, and they quickly accepted my proposal, sparing everyone, including my boss's boss, from additional meeting fatigue.

Be respectful and be ready to say the thing that needs to be said because you believe it needs saying. Don't shy away from conflict or adversity. I've found that my no-nonsense approach helps cut to the chase and get people moving even in the most political corporate cultures. Chances are, most of us are thinking the same thing. So just get it out there and get moving in a direction.

## Keep It Simple, Stupid

It never ceases to amaze me when folks act like they are trying to win a prize for the most convoluted way to say something. I've been known to talk around a topic myself, and I learned the key to effective communication is to keep it simple, stupid—KISS. That's an acronym you should tattoo on the back of your eyelids.

Conveying your point clearly and concisely is impressive. If you can't explain something to a fourth grader, you don't understand it well enough yourself. Speak plainly, speak directly, and for heaven's sake, get to the point. If you don't know the answer, simply say, "Great question! I'll look into this and follow up with you tomorrow."

## Quit Jawing and Practice Listening

Let's touch on listening. Most people think communication is all about getting your point across and everyone agreeing. Wrong. It starts with listening to understand. The successful project managers I've known were the ones who really practiced listening.

Notice I used the word "practice." In kung fu, practitioners train their sensitivity to sense the subtlest changes in body dynamics, a skill crucial for mastering techniques like chi sao. Similarly, when you actively listen—really listen, not just wait for your turn to speak—you develop a sensitivity to the nuances of communication. You learn things. When you're curious and patient, you recognize problems before they become disasters, understand what's really going on with your team, and give space for good ideas to bubble up.

Here's a tip: Next time someone's talking to you, actually pay attention. Focus, nod your head (even when not in person or on camera), and for goodness' sake, put your phone down. Don't just hear words while you're formulating your retort. Listen to what someone is saying. Ask questions if you need to and get clarification; it shows you're paying attention and, more importantly, that you care.

Remember, listening isn't just about being silent while someone else talks. It's about understanding. It's about remaining curious. And sometimes, it's about reading between the lines and hearing what isn't being said. Just as in kung fu, where sensing the unspoken tensions and movements of your partner is key, in communication, that's where the real finesse comes in.

## Fall Forward

In the world of project management, if you're not stumbling now and then, you're probably not moving fast enough. Failure and mistakes are as inevitable as a Monday morning, but it's how you handle them that sets you apart.

**Own the Outcome:** When a blunder happens under your watch, step in to own the outcome. You may or may not want to personally own the mistake, depending on cultural perspectives. Risk-averse cultures may prefer a less obvious approach. Regardless of who ends up owning the mistake, it's more impactful to acknowledge it (without assigning blame) and get everyone refocused on the plan to get back on track.

**Communicate With Candor:** Let your team and stakeholders know what went wrong and what's being done about it. Be as transparent as a freshly cleaned window. This builds trust and shows that you're more focused on solutions than excuses.

**Make Mistakes Magical:** The magic of mistakes is in the learning. Every blunder is a mini master class in what not to do next time. Document these lessons, share them with your team, and make them part of your normal process, thereby turning patches of quicksand into solid ground.

## You're in Sales, After All

You should always ensure your stakeholders understand how your project's success benefits them. You can bet your bottom dollar that when you're getting the cold shoulder, it's because they've lost sight of what's in it for them.

Maybe they're up to their eyeballs in other stuff they think is more important than your little slice of pie. Or, heaven forbid, something's changed, and your project's looking about as appealing as last week's meatloaf. Worse yet, maybe they think your project's a bag of microwave popcorn waiting to blow up in their faces. Or —let's not sugarcoat it—maybe you did something to ruffle their feathers.

Whatever the reason, your job isn't just to juggle tasks

and deadlines. You've got to play detective and figure out their angle. (And you thought this wasn't a sales job!)

## Parting Embers

Effective communication isn't just about what you say; it's about hearing what isn't said. Just as in kung fu, where sensitivity and balance are crucial, these elements are key to mastering project management. Here are some takeaways:

- **Become an Effective Storyteller:** Master the art of telling your project's story. Clear, honest communication can transform potential disasters into triumphs. Remember that perception is often reality.
- **Create a Plan but Include Flexibility:** Add flexibility in as part of your framework. Adapt your approach based on whether stakeholders agree, disagree, won't commit, or ghost you.
- **Trust in Trust:** Trust is your most valuable currency. Earn it consistently and spend it wisely to maintain credibility and influence.
- **If You See Something, Say Something:** Don't hesitate to speak up. Clear, direct communication can resolve tension and propel projects forward. Be the voice that cuts through the noise with respect and assertiveness.
- **Keep Things Clear:** Speak plainly and directly for the most effective communication.

If you can't explain it simply, you may not understand it well enough.
- **Zip It and Listen:** Effective communication starts with active listening. Pay attention to what is being said and what is left unsaid. Cultivate curiosity and patience to truly understand your team and stakeholders.
- **Lean Into Failures:** Embrace mistakes as learning opportunities. Own the outcome, communicate transparently, and turn missteps into stepping stones for improvement.
- **Don't Just Manage, Sell:** Ensure your project's benefits are well understood by tailoring your communication.

Master these principles to become a more effective project leader. Stay balanced, open, and communicative. Remember the lesson from chi sao: All the tactics in the world won't amount to a hill of beans if you don't apply them. Don't just memorize the tactics. Learn when to use them, how to adapt them to new circumstances, and have the guts to make the call, even when it's tougher than a $2 steak.

## NINE

## The Dynamics of Herding Cats

"None of us is as smart as all of us."

—Ken Blanchard

The room was dead silent. Everyone was throwing daggers with their eyes. After a mandatory break to let tempers cool, we returned to the table.

The division's revenue was in free fall, and customers were running as if from a burning building. Our mission —accepted under the threat of layoffs—was to create a new offering.

Everyone had opinions. Some shared, some withheld, and some expressed—shall we say—passion.

We were eyeballing one another like gunslingers at high noon. I got up, grabbed a marker, and slowly walked to the whiteboard. If I didn't get this right, I'd face a firing squad.

"We're done if we don't cook up something. We know that. We're all a little freaked out, right?" I paused to let everyone shift from the friction we all felt to some form of mutual agreement. By acknowledging the truth of the moment, I aimed to sweep away biases and give us a firm foundation.

"What we don't know is how to get where we want to go, and we don't have time to make informed decisions. That's not a fun place to be," I continued. "Rather than argue about how to fix the problem, let's step back and get clear on the problem. How would you describe our problem?"

Pragmatic as ever, Liu went first: "All of our customers are leaving."

"Yep, that's definitely a problem," I agreed. "Sienna, what do you think?"

Back and forth we went, discussing, debating, and digging at the problem until we all felt settled, as if we'd struck gold. The team had agreed on something meaningful in a constructive way. Trust had emerged, and the focused effort generated enthusiastic energy to carry on. By the end of that day, we had sketched out a new plan and could begin our new project, together, as a team.

## Managing Different Personalities Without Losing Your Sanity

Managing a project team is like trying to herd cats. Have you ever tried to get a cat to do something? How about dozens of them all at once? You've got some loners, some needy ones, and the ones that scratch your favorite chair just because they can. Unlike cats, however, you can't always resort to bribing people with treats or distract them with chasing laser pointers.

While it's generally a bad idea to generalize, there are a few stereotypical personalities you'll have to contend with:

**The Stubborn Mule:** This one's set in their ways. They'll resist change like the plague. Don't try to strong-arm them; it'll only make them dig in their heels deeper. Instead, use logic. Show them hard evidence that your way works better. If they have good reasons for not agreeing, you should listen. If they don't provide you with solid evidence to sway your outlook, it's best to agree to disagree. To accomplish the mission, you'll have to get commitment that they're in to do the job; otherwise, move them out and find an alternate.

**The Eager Beaver:** These folks are always ready, always volunteering. Sounds great, right? Wrong. They'll take on too much, then drown. You gotta keep an eye on them to make sure they're not biting off more than they can chew.

**The Silent Tortoise:** They never speak up in meetings. It's not that they don't have ideas; they do, and sometimes, they're good. You need to create an environment where they feel comfortable speaking up. And sometimes, just ask them directly. With proper support and an adaptive approach, these sincere shellbacks can be some of your star players.

**The Office Politician:** Slipperier than an eel, these rascals are all about playing games, making alliances, and climbing the corporate ladder. They can be useful allies, so long as you can stay on the right side of their agenda. Keep your friends close and your enemies closer, they say. Well, keep these ones closest.

**The Spinning Top:** Like a blender without a lid, these personalities are effective but messy. Sure, they get the job done, but not without flinging problems all over the walls and ceiling. These team members are high-energy but high-maintenance. They're powerful at their job, like chainsaws, but like chainsaws, they're also risky. They need a firm hand and clear direction, or they'll spin out of control, leaving a wake of mayhem behind. Keep 'em focused to ensure they work wonders, not woes.

**The Dreamer:** A walking brainstorm, these folks are brimming with ideas but short on focus. They're like a fireworks display of creativity—spectacular but scattered. In charge, they turn teams into jugglers at a circus, constantly shifting from one item to another. Without a steady hand, you'll be chasing dreams instead of results. Keep 'em grounded, or you'll be lost in the ring of what-ifs and maybes.

**The Bureaucrat:** This people are living, breathing rulebooks. They love procedures more than a cat loves a warm lap. Think of them as the gatekeepers of red tape, turning your project into a labyrinth of processes. They're inflexible, seeing the world in strict black and white. Navigate them by playing to their love of rules: Make them feel like the expert. It's about cleverly guiding them to help you, not hinder you. Patience and a bit of cunning are your best tools here.

**The Perfectionist:** These folks are like meticulous artists, taking forever on every stroke. They're obsessed with getting every detail just right, which sounds good on paper, but in reality, it's like waiting for paint to dry. Their quest for perfection often means missed deadlines and frustrated teams. Managing them is all about setting them up for success. Either you create lots of buffer around them to paint their masterpiece or set clear boundaries and remind them that sometimes, "good enough" is, well, good enough.

**The Seagull Supervisor:** Swooping in on a seaside breeze to snatch your snacks and poop on your head, these bothersome birds can make a mess of things in a hurry—and when you least need the distraction. I've found it's best to have an "offline" meeting with the boss to respectfully—and firmly—let them know their tactics are troublesome. If they can't (or won't) adjust their approaches, find out what they need and put in the extra effort to keep them at bay. These gulls are best viewed from a distance.

And there you have your regular zoo of workplace personalities. In the jungle of project management, handling people is like herding animals; it's possible, but you'll need to have a wide-eyed view, a keen ear, and a whole lot of patience.

## Building a No-BS Team Dynamic

Now that you know some of the personalities you might encounter, you need to know how to build and maintain an effective project team. To have an effective team, you gotta cut to the chase. You can't afford to mess around when trying to get things done on a deadline, or you're going to find out what cold, hard reality feels like—and fast. Building a no-BS team dynamic means building a platform of trust where a core part of your team can deliver results with little or no drama. How do you do that?

**Remember, Honesty Is the Best Policy:** I don't mean that you should tell Jim from accounting that his new haircut makes him look like a poodle. I mean honesty about the project. If something's not working, say it. If you're behind schedule, admit it. But being candid is not an excuse to be a jerk.

**Encourage Accountability:** Everyone screws up. It's part of being human. But if you make a mistake, own up to it. Don't try to pass the buck. That just creates an environment where no one trusts one another. High-trust teams pull together and help their members move through the problems to a solution.

**Foster Respect:** You don't have to like everyone, but you do have to respect them. That means listening when they talk, considering their ideas, and acknowledging their efforts. You also have to call out disrespect when you see it and set boundaries to ensure each team member is respected.

**Stay Curious:** The best way I've found to stay respectful and not get triggered is to stay curious. Ask questions and seek to understand genuinely why someone said what they said or did what they did. With that understanding, you can then move to a solution.

**Leave Your Ego at the Door:** This isn't about who's the smartest or who's got the best ideas. It's about getting the project across the finish line. Ego can be a great motivator when it's pointed at overcoming things. But ego can be damning when people get wrapped up in who's better than whom or they are too fragile to take criticism.

**Ditch the Jargon:** Speak plainly and directly. If you can say it in 10 words instead of 50, do it. Nobody's got time for a lecture. Jargon can be useful when it helps everyone get the point across efficiently. But when it starts to cloud the meaning of the message, it's time to ditch the jargon.

**Allow for Some Drama:** While a no- or low-drama team dynamic is ideal, it's not always realistic. A group of high-performance team members can carry the occasional high-maintenance team member and survive. When you find yourself forced to carry that person on your back, first focus on ensuring you explore whether you've missed a key means to leverage their skills. If, after thoughtful inventory, you conclude they are too heavy a load to bear, find a way to minimize their drag on the team's performance.

Ideally, your team dynamics are characteristic of your organizational culture. But that may not always be a luxury you have. High-performance teams may have to operate within broader cultures of risk aversion or outright politics. It's not ideal, but it can work. Your team can carve out a nice little existence for a time. In my experience, the more often your team wins, the more autonomy you'll get.

Remember, a team is only as good as its dynamics. A nononsense team isn't just good for the project; it's good for your soul. You'll find you enjoy coming to work more often. Even if you don't enjoy the work you're saddled with, you'll find the people you're riding with make it all worthwhile. If anyone tells you different, they're the ones who are full of it.

## Parting Embers

Project management is no walk in the park; it's more like herding cats while walking a tightrope. Every team is a blend of unique personalities, each bringing quirks and challenges. Here's what you need to remember to keep your sanity intact and your project on track:

- **Recognize Diverse Personalities:** Understanding and managing different personality types is crucial. From the Stubborn Mule to the Seagull Supervisor, each has its own ways and needs a tailored approach.
- **Build Trust:** Honesty, accountability, and respect are the bedrocks of a no-BS team dynamic. Be transparent about challenges, own up to mistakes, and respect each team member's contributions.
- **Stay Grounded and Curious:** Keep egos in check, speak plainly, and stay curious. A genuine interest in understanding others' perspectives fosters a collaborative environment.
- **Embrace Some Drama:** A little bit of drama is inevitable. Learn to manage it effectively, ensuring it doesn't derail the project. Focus on leveraging team members' strengths and minimizing their drag on performance.

Herding cats requires patience, a keen eye, and a lot of perseverance. Project management is never just about getting the job done; it's about how you get it done and who you bring along for the ride. Embrace the chaos, manage it well, and you'll build a team that's not just effective but a joy to work with.

# TEN

## Building Bridges Between Dreamers and Realists

"Vision without action is daydream; action without vision is nightmare."

—Japanese Proverb

Howie was at it again, waving his hands expressively as he regaled us with tales of last year's successes. "We crushed it!" Howie exclaimed. Then, leaning in and giving a dramatic pause, he said, "Here's where we're going this year."

As Howie maneuvered through his slides and grand plans to take over the world, Kyle began messaging me. "Here we go again. Another half-baked 'pivot' we'll have to juggle with everything else we're doing. <GROAN>."

Every project manager worth their salt has to contend with their fair share of dreamers and realists. Dreamers walk around with their heads in the clouds, while realists keep their eyes fixed on the ground.

## Dancing With Dreamers

Dreamers paint pretty pictures with their words, swaying listeners with visions of future glory, inconsiderate of present effort. Without the proper insulation, these visionaries begin to wear out their teams, skipping from idea to idea every month or quarter. Over a short amount of time, the rank-and-file grow weary of the grand plans that ultimately wind up going nowhere.

How do you handle pie-in-the-sky ideas without getting your wings burned?

We need the dreamers of our organizations. They help us see what is possible and think about a future state that promises something better than today. Yet their fire can burn our projects to the ground when proper firewalls are not installed. Your job in all this is getting stuff done. You've often got to work with executives who have a fuzzy idea of what they want. You'll have to ensure that is properly translated into actionable reality.

Channeling and grounding the dreamer's electricity takes patience for the pragmatic PM. Meanwhile, the visionary project manager must resist the temptation of following the visionary on a quest of the ages without considering the consequences.

Which one are you? Once you know, my advice is straightforward. Here's how to ally yourself with your dreamers and avoid getting caught up in the mirage:

**Listen Intently, Challenge Earnestly:** For the pragmatic PM, challenging is the easy part; it's the listening that may be hard to stomach. Remember not to immediately dismiss visions that don't seem practical. A dreamer can be a powerful ally and remind you what is possible along your journey.

For the visionary PM, listening is the easy part; it's the challenging you may find hard because the vision resonates with you. You must learn to ask realistic questions and challenge the dream. Stage the dreamer for a constructive conversation, then channel your most negative team member or boss and start throwing out daggers like they might pop the dream-filled balloon.

How's this going to work in the real world? What's the cost? The timeline? What is the downside in doing nothing? The truth is that dreams are free, but reality comes with a price tag. It's best to have an estimate of that price before you decide to buy in.

**Provide a History Lesson:** History can be a wonderful teacher. Show the dreamer how past projects flew too close to the sun and went down in flames. Ask them how their vision is different or will be implemented to succeed. Press them to think through the next level of details and circle back with you when they're ready.

**Run Parallel, Not Perpendicular:** Remember, don't try to shut the dreamers down directly, or they'll bristle and go over or around you. Instead, pull alongside them and work with them to understand their goals and objectives. Often, dreamers can be well-intentioned but suffer from a lack of practical pairing. They benefit from having someone who can implement their vision. If that isn't you, use your connections to help connect them with a person who can. You get them off your back, and they get to continue to work through their ideas with an ally. When the plan is more fully baked, then you can sink your teeth in.

**Try to Find the Golden Nugget:** Sometimes, these dreamers stumble upon a real gem. If you're chartered to help realize this dream, pursue prototypes and don't go gambling it all on a single bet. Iterate often, timebox everything, and get moving.

## Balancing Innovation with Practicality

Most folks you'll deal with on the project team are realists. If you're looking for encouragement, these folks can sometimes feel like a wet blanket on a cold night. They're all about the "been there, done that" and would rather play it safe than risk a new approach.

Mixing dreamers and realists can be a recipe for disaster. We need realists to get the job done. Yet without the dreamer's vision, realists will just keep doing the same old thing day after day.

**Encourage Embracing Change Without Falling Off the Cliff:** Realists typically groan when they see a dreamer coming. This is especially true if they've worked with them for any length of time. It might have become normal to nod their heads and smile out of a sense of common courtesy. Even as the words are leaving the dreamer's mouth, the realist is silently lighting a match to each and every one. Learn to read between the lines and assess why change threatens the realist. Do they need more information? Why do they feel threatened? Why are they disconnected? Which level of resistance is the realist operating at: They don't get it (and need more information), they don't like it, or they don't like the dreamer?

## The Art of Compromise

Your job is to bridge the gap between the dreamers and the realists, to find middle ground. Look for solutions that satisfy both camps—innovative yet actionable.

Make sure everyone knows the limits. Innovation is great, but not at the cost of blowing deadlines and budgets.

Remember, being a project manager is like being a ringmaster in a circus. You've got to keep the show going, regardless of the clowns and the high-wire acts. Keep the dreamers dreaming and the realists realistic, and somewhere in that mess, you'll find a way to get things done.

## Trust Is the Bridge

If you haven't figured it out already, trust is important. As I mentioned earlier, managing your trust bank is critical. When dealing with this dynamic, you'll have to be mindful of others' trust banks as well.

If either the pie-in-the-sky dreamers or the down-to-earth realists feel like their perspective isn't valued, moving your project forward is going to be harder than getting an old pickup truck out of a muddy ditch. Spinning wheels will sling sludge everywhere and make absolutely no difference in getting out. It's a frustratingly messy business, and all you end up doing is digging yourself in deeper. So make sure you're working to keep both sides earnestly engaged with each other in pursuit of a common goal.

## Be a Problem-Solver

Ensuring your teams are focused on a common goal means being aligned on the problem you're all fighting against. Getting and keeping projects on track requires a lot of problem-solving. If you don't know this yet, you will soon—if you stick with project management for any length of time.

It turns out that aligning stakeholders to a common problem and keeping the project on track through one problem after another is actually a fairly simple recipe. But it's not always an easy recipe to follow; everyone likes to wing it and jump straight to the solution. There's a lot more to solving a problem than simply thinking you know the outcome. This practiced approach has worked for me time and again:

**Document the Problem:** First, list what you think your problem is. Get clear on your problem statement before moving to the next step. Everyone should agree. If you haven't been doing this, you'll be amazed at the clarity this gives.

**Write All the Symptoms:** Then, list out the symptoms this problem is causing; circle back and compare your symptoms with your problem statement and see if you still agree that you wrote out the correct problem.

**Write All the Options:** If you're agreeable, list out all —I mean every—option for solving the problem; the more options you have, the better chances you'll have of solving it.

**Get Going:** Finally, pick an option and go with it. Get moving and stay moving by setting a timeline and assigning owners.

**Follow Up Regularly:** Make sure you follow up with this and keep using this recipe to get results.

This recipe works well solo or in a group setting and will give you focus. Remember, stay focused on the present step; don't fall for the temptations of racing ahead or getting stuck bellyaching about stuff that's out of your control. Mastering this simple recipe helps you to stand out in others' minds because of how well you manage through challenging issues. With enough practice, you'll start to see how it also lowers the level of friction throughout your life.

## Parting Embers

As you navigate the dynamic interplay between dreamers and realists in project management, you'll find balancing vision and practicality is what turns dreams into reality. Here are the key takeaways to keep your projects on track while maintaining harmony between these two forces:

- **Embrace Both Perspectives:** Acknowledge the value that both dreamers and realists bring to the table. Dreamers inspire innovation, while realists ensure feasibility.
- **Listen and Challenge:** Listen intently to dreamers and challenge their visions constructively. For realists, encourage them to consider new possibilities while grounding ideas in practicality.
- **Facilitate Collaboration:** Bridge the gap by facilitating open communication and collaboration between dreamers and realists. Help them see each other's perspectives and work towards a common goal.

Balancing the dreams of visionaries with the practicalities of realists is not just about compromise; it's about creating a synergy that drives successful project outcomes. Keep both sides engaged, respect their contributions, and steer the ship with a steady hand to navigate through the turbulent waters of project management.

## ELEVEN

## Saving the Day Ruins the Team

---

"The best executive is the one who has sense enough to pick good men to do what he wants done, and self-restraint enough to keep from meddling with them while they do it."

—Theodore Roosevelt

---

"SEVERITY 1 | Production Down," the notification read. Emails began to flood inboxes, and instant messaging channels turned bold, with bubbles popping up on computer screens around the world. Engineers quibbled among themselves like bees buzzing in a hive, attempting to posit where the problem could be. Directors interjected tidbits of obvious wisdom. Not to be left out, senior and executive vice presidents piped in with their own status update requests.

The session labored on. Jack listened for a while and eventually said, "The problem is related to the database—somehow." Senior engineers and even one director questioned how that could be. All the typical metrics were green, with no signs of distress. Jack continued to observe, quietly working in the background.

Precious minutes ticked by. Engineers began to fall silent, having expended the quiver of ideas they'd aimed at the problem. Nearly a dozen engineers and leaders sat there, frustrated and bewildered.

Then, like a bolt of lightning just before thunder, Jack's voice flashed. "The number of connections is exceeding the database server's capacity. It's a flaw in the code."

"How do you know that?" John asked.

"Wait, look at this. He's right," Bob said. "The server is getting overwhelmed with connection requests."

Jack's insight thundered through the room. "We weren't even watching that," came John's disappointed response as he shook his head.

The session carried on. It was 4 a.m. where Jack lived, and he'd been up all night.

"Jack, I know you need some sleep. Can you write this up and get your team to look at it when they get in?" I inquired.

"I'll need to solve the problem. My team can't do this," Jack replied shortly, leaving no room for argument.

And the next day, Jack saved the day again, all by himself. I could almost imagine him pulling apart his button-down shirt with both hands to reveal a secret "S" beneath.

## Superhero Syndrome

Jack had a well-earned reputation of being a superhero because he often rescued everyone from total obliteration. Everyone knew that when he was on the job, the problem would get handled. Management really didn't care about the how of it. They just knew he would make the problem disappear. His ability to make problems disappear led to a promotion that put him in charge of two teams. No question about it: Jack was a savior and a rainmaker.

But could Jack mentor a team into becoming superheroes themselves?

Problem-solving is a highly desired skill. Those who excel at it are often called upon to save the day. Whether it be a software developer, sales professional, or project manager, problem-solvers deliver results. Upper management often lavishes praise and glory on individual producers who deliver results. Once they've accumulated enough successes, management often taps these go-getters to see if they have what it takes to lead a team. But solving technical challenges as an individual contributor is far different from building and leading other gifted individuals.

Unlocking others' potential is a skill many technically gifted people misunderstand. They attempt to clone themselves or expect others to just "get it" like they did. It's common for them to get frustrated and smother their teams. After all, they can just do it better and faster themselves. In so doing, they fail to recognize allowing just a little oxygen in the room will allow the spark to ignite into a blazing fire of acumen and autonomy around them.

Project managers often find themselves in an even more precarious situation. With no direct authority over the teams they lead, PMs must rely on supreme interpersonal skills. In a culture where individual contributors are celebrated for getting stuff done and saving the day, a project manager's reputation is disproportionally tied to others' abilities to succeed.

This doesn't mean your destiny is without a measure of your control. First and foremost, your ability to guide the narrative is key. Beyond this, I encourage you to think less about yourself as a manager and grow into donning the mantle of leadership. A leader isn't defined by how many direct reports they have. Leaders guide a group in achieving a common goal. Leaders motivate and inspire others, set direction, and make decisions that influence the course of the group. Sounds a lot like what we've been talking about up to this point, doesn't it?

## Ask the Dumb Questions

How do you make space for others to grow? How do you lead others when you don't understand all the moving pieces yourself? While there are a host of different project leadership styles, I'll share what I found worked best for me.

I grew into leadership much the same way Jack did. I was always the go-to guy for a technical answer early in my career. Even during my early days as a manager, it never occurred to me to create space for others. I thought they would figure it out and step up or get out of the way. It wasn't until I first stepped into project management that I was confronted with a novel feeling: I didn't know everything anymore! I didn't like that feeling at all.

Over time, I learned that I needed to develop my ability to ask really good questions. Then it occurred to me that some of the best questions were the really dumb questions. It was so counterintuitive at first.

I needed to understand something very specifically. I had to explain it in simpler terms to upper management. I also needed to ensure I knew which technical resources to lobby for. So I asked a lot of questions. I'd repeat things experts would explain in simple paraphrases. They would offer confirmation or correction. Eventually, I got it.

Early in my tenure, my questions were very directed. If you imagine how two magnets interact with each other through invisible force, so too did my questions cause immediate and direct actions. I began to realize my impatience was driving questioning aimed at a solution much the same way Jack had directly solved the technical problems.

As I began to ask more open-ended questions, team members began filling the space I had left open. I found that as I asked fewer, more open-ended questions, team members would organically race ahead and offer responses nuanced in ways not present in earlier sessions.

As a few team members voiced their thoughts, other team members felt welcome to voice their own. I began to find that I wasn't the one asking so many questions. Meetings began to take on a tone like you'd hear when a group of friends gets together and talks about sports or the latest streaming series.

I had to get past my own ego, and I had to get comfortable asking the dumb questions. At first, I was tethered to the quid pro quo of solving problems and receiving praise. By asking the dumb questions, I nurtured my own confidence in guiding others to become heroes themselves. By learning to create space for others to breathe, I reinforced my confidence the problem would be solved while simultaneously strengthening others' confidence in themselves.

I discovered that by resisting the compulsion to unveil my own secret identity, I empowered others to become heroes in their own right. It turns out that as important as saving the day is, it's equally important others have the opportunity to play superhero, too. In this way, organizations foster growth and provide a scaffolding where saving the day doesn't ruin the team.

## Parting Embers

Project management can often feel like a high-wire act, where balancing immediate problem-solving with long-term team development is crucial. Remember, true leadership isn't just about saving the day; it's about empowering members of your team to become heroes themselves. Here's what helps you balance immediate success with lasting impact:

- **Let Your Team Own Things:** Encourage your team members to step up and take ownership of problems. By doing so, you foster a culture of growth and independence.
- **Ask Open-Ended Questions:** Move beyond directed inquiries. Open-ended questions create space for team members to think critically and contribute more meaningfully.
- **Resist the Hero Complex:** Avoid the temptation to solve every problem yourself. Allow your team to find solutions and grow from the experience.
- **Develop Interpersonal Skills:** Your ability to connect with and motivate your team is critical. Lead with empathy and clear communication.

- **Foster Confidence:** Build your team's confidence by trusting them with responsibilities and acknowledging their successes.

By empowering others, asking the right questions, and providing a supportive environment, real leaders cultivate a team of engaged adults who become strong, capable leaders in their own right and tackle challenges together.

## TWELVE

## Scope Creep: The Monster Ate My Deadline

"Focusing is about saying no."

—Steve Jobs

"We've got to have this new feature in two weeks!" Tim demanded. "We're signing up customers at the annual partner event and need to automatically select the correct pricing tier when we push this button." Tim moved the cursor on the shared screen, circling the area like water down a drain.

"You want us to extend this functionality so the partner can select these options in their portal instead of us doing it manually in ours. Is that right, Tim?" I clarified.

"Yes!" he confirmed.

"And this is worth … ?" I inquired.

"$350k U.S. in the first year, I estimate," Tim said.

"That seems like a fair ask to me. What do you think, Rob?"

Rob, our product owner, agreed with a quick nod.

"The only problem I have is timing, Tim. I'm already working on an issue for this partner and finishing other roadmap work that will keep my team busy until your deadline," I said.

There was a brief pause as both sides weighed their options silently. Tim knew two weeks was a tall ask, but he wanted a commitment that the work would get done.

"Tim, what's happening at this event in two weeks, exactly?" I inquired.

"Well, the partner is making several exciting announcements in their program and wants to announce this new educational and not-for-profit pricing," Tim explained, highlighting customer demand and market opportunity.

"Could we commit to delivering in our next release? That would be in two months," I offered.

Eager to negotiate, Tim countered with an expected response, "Could we do it in four weeks?"

"Good salespeople don't take no for an answer," I thought, cracking just a bit of a smile. "Tim, two months is the best we can do. You're welcome to escalate this if you disagree."

## Creepy Monsters

There's a beast more feared than a Monday morning without coffee: project scope creep. Constantly changing form and size, this monster crawls all over everything and everyone like a zombie fungus devouring budgets, brains, and deadlines whole.

Scope creep is the leading cause of projects not delivering value. It's a never-ending story of "just one more thing" and exemplifies human psychology at its finest. Temptation is often too great for most, and through a lack of organizational and leadership discipline, the original intention of the project is corrupted and lost. Abject failure is often only recognized in a rearview filled with the remorse of "would've, could've, should've."

Scope creep usually starts innocently enough. A small request here, an "Oh, wouldn't it be nice if ... " there. But give it an inch, and it'll take a mile, leaving your project bloated, over budget, and behind schedule.

Picture this: You're working on what was supposed to be a straightforward website redesign. Suddenly, someone wants a new feature, then another, and another. Next thing you know, you're not just redesigning a website; you're building the digital platform with designs rivaling the likes of Amazon.

There are a few ways to handle scope creep. Obviously, the most common is to do nothing, which is the entire reason projects go south and why this chapter exists.

Since most of us are not that masochistic and actually want to deliver timely value, we'll move on to the more desirable methods of managing scope creep.

**Change This:** The age old "change request" is a tried-and-true tradition in project management. It presents a formal method to request scope changes. While this sounds easy enough, change requests must come with consideration of the larger impact on the iron triangle and original project intent. While adding an extra rung on a ladder may be one thing, changing the deliverable to a staircase or an elevator changes the intention and effort altogether. So change request processes must be robust and considerate of a PM's overarching mandate to "get it done on time and on budget."

**Rainy-Day Buffer:** If you've ever had unexpected car troubles, a sick pet, or an emergency room visit, you know how much it hurts the wallet. After a few unexpected emergencies like this, you start to get wise and squirrel away funds to help when unexpected expenses come up. Similarly, seasoned PMs build in buffer resources to accommodate varying levels of scope changes. They've been around enough to know things come up. The upside of this approach is that it always impresses folks when you can pull a minor miracle out of your back pocket.

**Agile Versus Reality:** Agile project methodologies evolved out of a recognition that life happens and people can't make up their minds. Whether it was under the auspice of "frequent delivery" or simply a way of maintaining sanity in the face of indecisive leadership, the core principles of Agile make sense in certain contexts. Success comes when project leadership can successfully align the way in which a project is managed with what the business needs to keep going. In particular, software development projects can realize shorter value-delivery cycles with a continuous delivery mindset. But be warned: Agile won't solve all your problems and can quickly inflict whiplash on delivery teams without managing proper discipline.

**Just Say "Instead":** "Instead" can be stronger than "yes" and nicer than "no." Rather than channeling the Nancy Reagan "Just Say No" campaign of the 1980s, you can counter with, "I can't do this. Instead, I can do that." After all, being "Doctor No" doesn't win you a lot of friends or encourage others making deposits into your trust bank. Likewise, saying "yes" all the time won't get you across the finish line. While you don't have to accept every change in scope that comes your way, Agile methods offer some important insights into tradeoffs. I've not seen this work well in one-off projects, but when organizations are built for sequential delivery (such as products or services delivery), a PM can negotiate a solid position to deliver upon the request in a later cycle. This keeps the current project on track, gets the stakeholder what they want (eventually), and teaches resource discipline simultaneously.

## Ego Monsters

Now let's talk about egos—the silent fuel of scope creep. You've got stakeholders who think their every whim is gospel, and team members who get too attached to their ideas. The key to managing these characters? Communication and backbone. Don't be a yes-man. Be clear about what's feasible and what's fantasy. Remember, while flattery might earn you a pat on the back, it won't protect your project from morphing into the many-headed Hydra of Greek mythology.

How do you keep this monster at bay?

## The Eisenhower Matrix

First, get everyone used to making decisions using the Eisenhower Matrix. President Dwight D. Eisenhower made famous the quote, "I have two kinds of problems, the urgent and the important. The urgent are not important, and the important are never urgent." Yet as famous as this is, I'm always shocked at how often colleagues look like deer in headlights when I ask them if a change is urgent or important.

Decisions can be evaluated using two pairs of criteria: important/unimportant and urgent/not urgent. Once they are graded, they can then be placed in one of four quadrants in an Eisenhower Matrix, or Urgent-Important Matrix.

Here's how it breaks down:

**Urgent and Important (Do It Now):** These tasks are like a house on fire. If you don't deal with them now, you'll have bigger problems soon.

**Important but Not Urgent (Schedule It):** This is the stuff that'll build your future, like planning or improvement projects. Important, yes, but it doesn't have to be done this minute. Schedule it before it becomes a fire.

**Urgent but Not Important (Delegate It):** These are the pesky little tasks that keep you busy but don't really contribute to your goals. Hand them off to someone else if you can. I often find building out playbooks and processes greatly help to curb these types of priorities. By asking, "What can we do differently next time?" seeking consensus, and enforcing accountability, you'll find these issues start to fade.

**Neither Urgent Nor Important (Dump It):** This is just clutter. If it's not urgent and it's not important, why the heck is it on your plate? Really look at why you're hanging on to it. Most of the time, you should just toss it out and don't look back.

With practiced use, you'll find a kind of shorthand. I promise you this will change the way your organization thinks about change. I've single-handedly forced this in organizations as a product manager when managing feature backlog, and it has unequivocally been the single biggest factor in helping maintain sanity while driving productivity.

| The Eisenhower Matrix | |
|---|---|
| **Do It Now:**<br>*Urgent + Important* | **Schedule It:**<br>*Important + Not Urgent* |
| **Delegate It:**<br>*Urgent + Not Important* | **Dump It:**<br>*Not Urgent + Not Important* |

## Guard Your Boundaries

Another common gap in managing scope creep is porous boundaries. To keep this monster at bay, you must honor and enforce clear boundaries like they're the law. The way you do this is through understanding the culture as well as the organization's goals and desires in delivering the project. Once understood, you can then better align and combat unnecessary scope changes. I recommend treating scope creep as if it were Starbucks coffee—burnt-tasting and expensive as a regular habit!

This is generally the point where folks start thinking I'm advocating for one project delivery methodology over another. I'm not. Boundaries don't equal Waterfall, just like no boundaries don't equal Agile. Each framework has its benefits.

Waterfall is step by step, linear, like following a recipe. Finish one step before you move to the next. Waterfall projects generally have a longer cycle time that makes scope changes both tempting and riskier. This becomes challenging when today's customers hunger for value delivery more quickly than getting a Big Mac combo.

Agile became a popular alternative for just this reason; the methodology acknowledges how frequently priorities shift in today's culture. Agile is iterative and adaptable. You do a little bit, check if it works, and then adjust. Yet Agile has its own problems. If the organization isn't disciplined in its focus and rigorous in its decisioning, it will incur incredible switching taxes that I've seen result in launch delays, misfiring value delivery, and team burnout.

Regardless of the organizational approach to managing project delivery, be disciplined enough to align scope changes to your cycle times and ensure decision-makers are trading enough to offset the cost of the change.

Managing scope creep isn't for the faint-hearted or flimsy-willed. It's a skill, an art, and you gotta have a little bit of a street fight in you. In the battleground of project management, victory is achieved in each and every skirmish along the way. Keep egos and boundaries in check, overcommunicate, force decisions, and stay vigilant.

## Parting Embers

Scope creep is the monster under the bed, waiting for a chance to devour your deadlines. Here's how you keep this beast at bay and your project on track:

- **Control Change:** Align to how you and your team want to manage the change control process. A robust process helps keep the project focused.
- **Build Buffers:** Plan for the unexpected by building buffer resources into your schedule and budget. This prepares you to handle unforeseen changes without derailing the project.
- **Use Agile Wisely:** Being agile doesn't magically save the day. Agile methods can help manage changing priorities, but they require discipline. Align project management with business needs to maintain a steady course.
- **Negotiate Instead:** Rather than saying "no" outright, offer alternatives. This approach helps balance stakeholder demands with project feasibility and maintains good relationships.
- **Control Egos:** Manage stakeholder and team member egos by being clear about what is feasible. Strong communication and backbone are essential.

Managing scope creep isn't just about saying "no" to every request outside the original parameters; it's about steering the project with a firm but flexible hand. Your ability to manage changes effectively defines your success. Stay disciplined, communicate clearly, and keep your focus on delivering value. Your reputation and your project depend on it.

THIRTEEN

# The Whoosh and Thud of Deadlines

---

"I love deadlines. I love the whooshing noise they make as they go by."

—Douglas Adams

---

The market research division's revenue had plummeted by 63%, and customer retention was now at a dismal 40%. In our eleventh hour, Ted, our CEO, convened our research team for a two-day workshop.

"Things are bad. I brought you all here to work together to see if there is a solution," Ted solemnly opened. "The way we've been doing things isn't working. I'm going to step out and let you brainstorm solutions without interjecting my bias. If you have questions or need input, I'll be in my office."

After Ted closed the door, we sat in stunned silence. Some hung their heads; others searched their colleagues' eyes for acknowledgment. As for me, I had questions.

Through a series of conversations, a plan began to take shape. Chief among our problems were the quality and timeliness of our deliverables. We were inconsistent, and the quality didn't encourage customers to renew their services.

After much back and forth, we realized we needed to establish a deliverable cadence. We aligned on daily, weekly, monthly, and quarterly content drops, each with different expectations for quality and rigor. Work was divided among the team, with larger "think pieces" supported by everyone.

This cadence of deadlines forced clarity regarding our critical path. To my surprise, it also became a rallying cry, unifying the team around a common goal. A few wins turned into many. Over the next year, we stabilized revenue, improved customer retention, boosted team morale, and dramatically increased sales win ratios.

It turns out deadlines are a crucial ingredient for project and program success.

## The Sound of Deadlines

I've always thought deadlines have a kind of "sound" as they come and go. Whoosh! Some deadlines go zipping by so fast that I feel their wind on my cheek. Some deadlines are so high-friction, they sound like sweaty flesh sticking to a vinyl seat in a Mississippi summer. I've had a few deadlines screech like kids watching a horror movie. Yet other deadlines make an unceremonious thud, as if a pallet of concrete just squashed any hope I had of success.

Over time, I recognized the sounds I imagine relate to how I feel the project is progressing. When scope is well-defined and things are moving along, I hear the steady tick-tock of a grandfather clock. In recognizing this, I discovered how I could help others navigate their own conflicts with a deadline.

People have a peculiar relationship with deadlines. You see, deadlines require commitment. It's been my observation that many experience anxiety around commitments. I have found a few common anxieties that, when understood, serve to encourage and coax the very best from your team and stakeholders. Here are the most common hang-ups I've had to navigate:

**Eating the Elephant:** Many times, folks just don't understand how to approach the problem because it's too big. I'll certainly confess to this myself. This phrase is used to describe how to take a big problem and break it down into smaller bites so it can be more easily digested. Failure to deliver a dependency may block your project from successfully concluding. When someone struggles with this, it's important to come together and work through deconstructing the problem into its smaller parts. Then a more understood plan can be enacted.

**Too Busy:** Sometimes, the most well-meaning person may just have too much going on. They aren't making a task a priority, and it's blocking your project deadline. To resolve this, start by pulling the person aside, convey the importance of the matter, and pursue a commitment to deliver. If they can't deliver or won't commit, start looking for alternatives to get the proper support.

**Fear of Failure:** Deadlines often evoke fear of failure in individuals. The commitment to meet a deadline can trigger anxiety about not living up to expectations, whether these are personal standards or external requirements. This fear might not be about the commitment itself but about the consequences of failing to meet the commitment. When confronted with this type of fear, help the individual recognize the fear and feel psychologically safe. Understand what accommodations may be needed. If they are reasonable, do what can be done. If they are not, it may be time to register a risk and evaluate options.

**Perfectionism:** For perfectionists, deadlines can be particularly daunting because they impose a finite time to achieve a task perfectly. The commitment to a deadline might exacerbate fears about making mistakes or producing work that does not meet their high standards. As a recovering perfectionist myself, I find it necessary to constantly remind myself what is required and what is instead nice to have. My high standard of quality may not always be required to achieve success within the timeline or budget provided.

**Procrastination:** Some individuals struggle with procrastination and time management, which can put deadlines at risk. The commitment required to meet a deadline highlights these challenges and can lead to avoidance behaviors. In such cases, helping the individual with achievable milestones and regular check-ins may be the way to see reasonable success. But if the person continues to struggle, the conversation may turn toward whether the person is truly committed to the project's success.

**Uncertainty of Change:** Committing to a deadline means locking in a course of action, which can be intimidating for those who fear change or the unknown. The commitment reduces flexibility and requires one to confront whatever task or decision is at hand. First understand why the individual fears the change. Next, I've found it can be reassuring to align teams to "fallback positions"—an age-old military defense tactic allowing teams to retreat to a more defensible position when the current position is overrun. This has proved to be a useful tactic to reassure this person that if the worst happens, a safety net will catch them.

## To Timebox or Not to Timebox

Balancing "iron variables" in the equation of a project requires simultaneously considering the outcome and its primary components—scope and budget across time. With the end always in mind, savvy project managers ask the ever-present question, "What's standing between me and my next milestone?"

Ideally, trusting your team to execute is the way. However, for the many reasons listed—and more—individuals seem to get stuck and need help. Your solution to this obstacle is through facilitation and support to get any wayward stakeholders out of the mud and back on the road to success. This often requires you to ladder up and down the levels of work to ensure forward progress is always maintained. More directly, you must interchangeably be able to talk technical with the team and strategy with the executives.

What's this got to do with timeboxing, you ask? Timeboxing—the act of allocating fixed and realistic deadlines to specific events or milestones—becomes a measure of value and progress as well as a method to provide clarity.

How much time do I need to get this done? Am I on time? Am I late?

Time certainly can feel like an enemy—always against us, pressuring us, cheating us. Yet in project terms, timeboxing is a tool that aids us in getting clear on scope, budget, risk, quality, and—yes—time remaining. Thinking in this way has the effect of moving things along or shining a spotlight on problem areas. Setting time limits on meetings requires you to focus on agenda. Setting milestone dates requires you to collaborate and push other things aside. Committing to project delivery dates helps clarify everyone's expectations. This discipline creates momentum through choice, propelling your project forward.

It is time that creates value through forcing us to sacrifice one path for another. Without choice, we face failure and regret.

## Timeboxing Is Not a Weapon

I've seen my share of folks who use timeboxing as a weapon. They set arbitrary deadlines seeking to manipulate and bludgeon others into submissive compliance.

Time's a beast we all gotta wrestle with on projects. Timeboxing is meant to help keep the monster at bay and give us some rails to run along so we're not just wavering in the wind. What I've found is that bookending projects with time ensures people don't feel any sense of priority in achieving a goal. That is, their objective just hangs around aimlessly at the bottom of a to-do list like an unmatched sock in the dryer. Status updates tend to sound like a broken record of "Oh, I haven't had time to get to it yet."

Superficial deadlines shouldn't be aimed at creating urgency unless the urgency is real. Don't use time as a weapon against your team. Instead, time should be viewed as a constraint the team faces together.

I've been amazed at the results I get when I sit down with my team and collaboratively work with them to commit to a deadline of their choosing. I don't make up a deadline. Instead, I align the team to a commitment, sanity-test their assertions, then hold them accountable to their commitment.

## Tactics for Hitting Tight Deadlines

Now for the meat of the matter: dealing with deadlines that are tighter than a drum. Here's my no-nonsense advice:

**Prioritize Like Your Job Depends on It (Because It Does):** Detail the knowns to be done and the unknowns needing answers, then hack away at the list like you're chopping wood. Focus on what matters most. Everything else can take a hike.

**Delegate Details:** You've got a team. Use it. Delegate like you're king of the hill, but make sure you're not just throwing tasks over the fence. Match tasks to skills, and don't micromanage.

**Speak Up:** Keep everyone in the loop. If you're headed for a blocker, speak up. Problems don't age well, like that leftover tuna sandwich in the break room fridge.

**The Art of the Shortcut:** Find quicker ways to do things, but don't cut corners that'll come back to haunt you. Automate the mundane, and remember, sometimes good enough is just that—good enough.

**Expect the Unexpected:** Plan for things to go wrong—because they will. When they do, don't panic. Fall back to your next defensible position and keep going.

**Commitment Is Crucial:** Ensuring that all team members are on the same page and fully committed to meeting deadlines is essential. Negotiation plays a significant role in this process, as there might be technical difficulties or uncertainties regarding the project's scope. Nonetheless, it's vital that everyone involved reaches a mutual agreement on the deadlines and is held accountable for managing contributions accordingly.

For better or worse, deadlines keep us on our toes. Balancing quality with timely delivery is like juggling flaming chainsaws—tricky, but not impossible. Remember to encourage your team through hard challenges. Agree upon delivery, and work through challenges one at a time. A regular cadence and shared success will build your team's confidence into an unstoppable juggernaut.

## Parting Embers

Time is the singular nonrenewable resource. Thus, deadlines are not just dates on a calendar; they're pivotal moments that define your project's success and your team's morale. Here are the key takeaways to master the art of deadlines:

- **Set Realistic Deadlines:** Timeboxing isn't about arbitrary dates. It's about setting realistic, meaningful deadlines that drive clarity and progress.

- **Understand Commitment Anxiety:** Identify and address the common fears and anxieties your team might have around deadlines, from fear of failure to perfectionism.
- **Prioritize and Delegate:** Break down large tasks, prioritize effectively, and delegate details to the right team members to maintain momentum.

Deadlines inspire anxiety but action as well. Balance quality with timely delivery by encouraging your team, agreeing on deliverables, and tackling challenges together and watch your team's confidence—and successes—grow.

FOURTEEN

## Real Money Really Matters

"When I was young I thought that money was the most important thing in life; now that I am old I know that it is."

—Oscar Wilde

It was my first business project since leaving the Marine Corps, and I was eager to make my mark. After authorizing a $350-per-hour service call for a DEC VAX supermini computer consultant to service an old, impact printer, I realized it was time to modernize our infrastructure. I scoped an ambitious project to modernize our entire approach to printing, including digitizing assets and upgrading the device fleet. Leadership was excited because it fit perfectly into our Lean Six Sigma program, offering opportunities to reduce sunk costs while increasing productivity.

Everyone was thrilled—everyone except Ronnie, our corporate controller. I chose my vendor-partner to manage the entire engagement and worked through the numbers to present to Ronnie. Before the project could be authorized, I had to convince Ronnie to switch from the company's traditional capital expenditure model, which required corporate approval, to an operating lease that could be taken as a monthly expense.

I'll never forget the day I proudly strolled into Ronnie's office to discuss my project proposal. "Of course, the numbers make sense," I thought. We could increase productivity and finally step out of the Dark Ages with modern technology! What's not to agree with?

I sat down across from Ronnie. He paused his work and leaned into his high-backed leather chair. He folded his thick fingers and began to rub his University of Tennessee college ring, looking up at the ceiling behind me. He didn't mince words. He turned his eyes to me and, in his slow Tennessean drawl, asked the toughest question I've ever heard: "Who you gonna fire?"

"Fire?" I sheepishly asked. I wasn't expecting any real resistance—certainly not this question.

"Yeah. Your budget includes assumptions about savings from 'soft dollars,'" Ronnie explained. "Unless you're going to fire 2 1/2—let's call it 3—people, this boat don't float."

"Soft dollars?" I asked.

He swiveled and leaned forward toward me, his elbows perched on the desk. Looking just over his folded fingers, Ronnie explained, "Payroll is money we actually spend. Every time I pay for service on one of those blasted printers, that's a check I have to write. Those are 'hard dollars.'"

I nodded in understanding.

He continued, "Productivity increases aren't direct savings unless you can prove you're applying them somewhere. I bet you dollars to donuts that if you gave Cassie an extra four hours in her day, she'd just play solitaire or powder her nose more often. That's not saving me anything. I want real savings, so if you want me to greenlight this project, tell me which three people you want me to fire."

I thought I was the white knight rushing in to save the day with my modernization project, but I walked out of Ronnie's office dragging my stomach on the floor. I had been exposed to the grim reality of how executives often think about project budgets. Ronnie had dropped a reality check on my head heavier than a 2-ton anvil. He wanted to know, "Where's the beef?"—aka the real savings.

I still wince thinking about that humbling experience to this very day. Ronnie was a tough-love teacher who taught me many lessons about how finance works. The lesson that stuck with me the most is that real money really matters.

## Tactics for Managing Budgets

In the battleground of business, it's not just about having a shiny new toy or being the hero who drags the company kicking and screaming into the 21st century. It's about making the numbers add up to a story that the bean counters can get behind. Real money talks, and everything else walks.

There's a plethora of project books that can teach you how to budget and estimate costs. Rather than revisit those practical tidbits, I'd like to share some pivotal tactics that made the difference during my time in the trenches:

**Learn the Language of Finance:** A common pitfall for PMs is not aligning their project proposals with the financial goals and metrics that matter to decision-makers. I walked into Ronnie's office speaking the language of productivity and modernization, but Ronnie was speaking the language of finance. It's like trying to play chess with checkers rules; sure, you're moving pieces around the board, but you'll never win the game. Frame the conversation how your stakeholder wants to hear it.

**Avoid Shiny-Object Syndrome:** In my eagerness to drag the company out of the Dark Ages, I fell prey to the shiny-object syndrome—chasing after the latest and greatest whizbang without fully considering everyone's perspective on the problem. PMs often make the mistake of advocating for new technologies or methodologies simply because they're new, not necessarily because they're right for the project. While the project wound up being a success, I didn't consider the counter-arguments to my lofty schemes. Ronnie was rightly gauging whether I was after the equivalent of a sports car when what the company really needed was a reliable minivan.

**Understand Financial Levers:** Stakeholders often get starry-eyed about the potential savings from new technologies or processes. They throw around terms like "efficiency gains" and "cost avoidance" like campaign taglines. But when push comes to shove, these savings are about as substantial as a politician's promise. It is important for PMs to discern the levers of the project budget. Whether the project is funded through cost offsets, discretionary funding, or discreet funding, there's nothing more jarring than reaching the end of an imaginary race you thought was far longer. Stay close to executive stakeholders and keep your eyes on the financial tea leaves.

**Consider Cash Flow Versus Budget:** PMs frequently make the error of focusing on the project's overall cost without considering how project expenditures will be affected by company cash flow. I'll never forget the time I went to pay for a new primary research vendor to start a research project, only to have the CFO tell me there wasn't any money to pay the vendor. We had funding from the customer, but the company had misappropriated funds elsewhere, placing the entire project in jeopardy.

**Never Ignore the Humans:** I was blindsided by the "Who you gonna fire?" question because I didn't understand how those controlling the purse strings thought about real money and real people. Whether it's layoffs, retraining, or changes in workflow, every project decision has a human impact; failing to account for that is like skipping the foundation when attempting to build a house. Get aligned to how project funders think about money and people.

**Know Your Role:** Remember, a project manager's job isn't to be the hero with all the answers; it's to navigate the messy, complex web of project constraints without getting caught in the sticky bits. Most times, that means listening more than talking. You can learn the most from people who ask you the hardest questions.

## Parting Embers

Walking the precipice of project budgets is like treading a narrow ledge; balance is crucial, and the stakes are high. Here's what to keep in mind to ensure your project stays financially sound and strategically aligned:

- **Align With the Finances:** Understand and attune your project proposals with the financial metrics that matter to decision-makers. Frame your conversations to match the priorities of your stakeholders.
- **Beware the Latest Fads:** It's tempting to pursue a new fandangled technology, but

always evaluate whether it truly meets the project's needs. Consider all perspectives before advocating for new solutions.

- **Understand the Actual Versus the Potential:** Recognize the difference between potential savings and actual, tangible financial benefits. Stay attuned to the financial strategies and constraints of your project.
- **Mind Potential Financial Gaps:** Keep a close eye on how project expenditures align with the company's cash flow to avoid financial surprises that could jeopardize your project.
- **Remember the People Part:** Every financial decision has a human consequence. Understand how budget changes could affect the people involved and navigate these challenges with empathy and foresight.

Your role isn't just to deliver results but to do so with strategic insight and human consideration. Master the financial landscape, and you'll not only drive successful projects but also build a legacy of trust and respect with peers and executives alike.

## FIFTEEN

## Chasing Quality: When Perfection Paralyzes Progress

"Perfection is the enemy of progress."

—Winston Churchill

"There is no way we'll ever meet all of these requirements," I said to Lynda with a sigh.

Looking at five pages of high-level requirements spanning architecture, cost control, management, and security, my head slumped, almost hitting my desk. The gap analysis alone would take weeks to complete. We'd never get the software up to corporate standards without an army of developers and testers. Who knew where we'd get the budget?

Lynda unwavering eyes indicated she was unfazed. She simply replied, "It's not realistic for us to do all of this work this week, this month, or even this year. What we need is a plan to get there."

It was obvious she'd danced to this tune many times before. She understood the game that needed to be played. She encouraged me to aim for the perfect standard but not get lost in the minutiae along the way.

"What can you get done with the resources you have for each release?" she probed.

"Well, I could start with … " I began, offering one thought, then another, and another. My list of priorities became clearer with each point I uttered. As if all at once, the fog of hesitation and doubt lifted, and I began to see a path forward.

## The Mask of Perfection

There is no such thing as the perfect project. Scope, cost, and time work together as legs supporting the tabletop of quality. These constraints are always competing with one another. When we hold perfection as the goal, it diminishes the importance of scope, cost, and time. This leads to unattainable outcomes, anxiety, and ultimately failure.

For perfectionists, quality can become a kind of mask to hide behind. Nothing except the very best will do, so nothing ever gets done because how could it ever be good enough?

## Tactics for Prioritizing Progress Over Perfection

How do we surmount this need to prioritize an unparalleled quality that only comes at the expense of success? These tactics will help you move from paralysis to action:

**Remember Quality Is Subjective:** For the perfection-focused individual, you must first accept that quality is a subjective perception. While it's useful to have a certain sense of ownership over each project you lead, you do not own your projects or the outcomes. You are a Sherpa, guiding your customers to a successful summit. As long as the outcome is safe and holds to ethical standards, it is their view of quality that ultimately matters —not yours.

**Get Clear on the Outcome:** You gotta cut through opaque layers and get to the heart of the matter. A seasoned PM knows to ask refining questions. Getting clear on the outcome means getting specific enough to know what the next step in your journey has to be.

**Prioritize the List:** Effectively manage tasks by distinguishing among urgent, important, and nice to have. Prioritize focusing on what significantly contributes to long-term success, adjusting as project dynamics change. This approach helps in dedicating time and resources to high-impact tasks.

**Run One Step at a Time, Not the Whole Race:** Forget about winning the marathon on your first day. Concentrate on not tripping over your own feet. When you get too fixated on the race, it's easy to get stalled by the project's entirety. Instead, break down larger milestones into smaller, manageable tasks. Focus on completing each task well before moving to the next, fostering a sense of accomplishment and maintaining momentum through incremental progress.

**Pursue Relentlessly:** Set a clear and compelling objective that guides all project decisions. Keep this ambitious yet achievable goal as your focal point, motivating your actions and ensuring alignment with the project's ultimate aims, despite potential obstacles.

**Know When to Pivot:** Be ready to make shifts in direction when necessary. Recognizing the need to pivot is key to adapting to new information or conditions, keeping the project on track toward its goals.

Incorporating these tactics into your project management approach can significantly enhance your ability to balance the pursuit of quality with the necessity of making progress. In implementing these tactics, you can lead your projects to success with agility and adaptability without getting paralyzed by the pursuit of perfection.

## Parting Embers

You should always strive to balance quality with progress. Progress over perfection is the key to successful project management. Here are the main takeaways to keep your projects moving forward without getting bogged down by the pursuit of perfection:

- **Quality Is in the Eye of the Beholder:** Understand that your definition of quality might differ from that of your stakeholders. Guide them toward a successful outcome that meets their standards, not just yours.
- **Get to the Heart of the Matter:** Focus on what truly matters by asking refining questions. Get specific about what needs to be done next to make meaningful progress.
- **Prioritize Toward Progress:** Distinguish between urgent, important, and nice-to-have tasks. Focus on what significantly impacts long-term success.
- **Take It One Step at a Time:** Break down larger milestones into smaller, manageable tasks. Celebrate each completed task to maintain momentum.
- **Think Big, Start Small:** Keep an ambitious yet achievable goal in sight as a guide to making all project decisions.
- **Maintain Flexibility:** Be ready to change direction when necessary. Adapt to new information or conditions to keep the project on track.

It's not about achieving perfection on the first try—or ever, really; it's about making steady, deliberate progress. By focusing on these tactics, you'll lead your projects to success without being paralyzed by the need for perfection.

## SIXTEEN

## Flying in Uncertain Skies: Mastering Risk and Resilience

"Security is mostly a superstition. Life is either a daring adventure or nothing."

—Helen Keller

"Shut it down. Shut it all down."

The call came down midmorning from 3rd Marine Aircraft Wing command to power down all our email servers. The Melissa virus had spread throughout the U.S. Marine Corps' newly transitioned email server network. Our server activity lights flickered with abandon, signaling an unprecedented spike in activity even before we reached the console.

Our server queues flooded with malicious emails promising "sexxxy.jpg" and "naked wife" faster than we could clear them out. It seemed the temptation was far too great for virile, young men with little cybereducation to resist.

Every opened attachment triggered a new rash of problems. Within hours, nearly all the Corps' 7,500 email servers were impacted, crippling messaging traffic for nearly three days as we worked feverishly to identify and fix the issues.

Like our civilian counterparts, we had become dependent on email to transmit and receive daily instructions. Without these messages, command staff down to the enlisted were left foundering.

By day three, our commanding officer had enough. Helicopters weren't flying missions.

"Pick up the damn phone!" our colonel screamed at the walls as he barreled down the halls with adjutant staff scurrying behind.

"Does no one remember what we did before emails, for crying out loud?" he roared, red-faced and fuming. "Get those birds in the air!"

As if a fog lifted, officers shook off the haze of the technological uncertainty and sprang into action.

We learned valuable lessons that week. First, risk is a constant, and you're never truly safe. Second, always have a Plan B. Finally, stay focused on the mission, not the methods.

## Lions and Tigers and Birds, Oh My!

Project managers don't typically think about risks like they are opportunities the same way entrepreneurs rattle off inspirational quips exalting "Carpe diem." In fact, I can't recall having met any project managers who enjoyed managing project risks. Risks are things to be avoided and mitigated at all times.

I confess, I've been party to quite a bit of handwringing about risk planning in my past. It took a lot of—ahem—exposure therapy to finally recognize a handful of tactics that enables me to cope with risks without losing my marbles. I'll share the important bits learned the hard way to help crystalize your thinking and hopefully give you the jump on your own learning.

**Safety Isn't Real:** To me, risk is a horizon. I can remember standing on the ocean shore in Southern California looking into the seemingly endless void of the nighttime sea. It appeared to span forever into a blackness I could palpably feel in the pit of my stomach. Meanwhile, behind me was the safety of lights and land. As I forced myself to stare out into that dark horizon, I soothed myself with the knowledge that I could always turn around. I came to realize that safety was simply the difference in my perception of the unknown. Similarly, as we look out over our own risk horizon, we see that one direction offers safety, while the other promises nothing but uncertainty. The very nature of project management is to impose control in pursuit of an outcome. It runs counter to uncertainty. Yet, when you recognize that safety isn't real and you face uncertainty, it helps you navigate the anxiety of your own risk horizon and plow forward under steady steam as you chart the course to your goal.

**Uncertainty Is Unknowable:** The very nature of uncertainty makes it unknowable. I've seen many people get wrapped up in analysis paralysis thinking on all the ways something could go wrong. A salty project manager can face uncertainty by simply shutting off the amygdala and refocusing on what is controllable and knowable. It's not ignoring the unknown, but rather honoring the fact that we are only ever equipped with a fraction of knowledge in our decisions. Yes, there are measures of control, but ultimately embarking on a project is to acknowledge a level of risk and proceed anyway.

**Knowing Is Half the Battle:** Like a favorite cartoon of mine always used to say, if you know it, you're already halfway to winning the battle. You don't have to like risk to manage it; you just gotta know how to get through it. Known risks can be more readily managed and mitigated. But when you don't know the specific risks that may come up, you'll need time to work through them. Like the extra room you make for Thanksgiving dinner by strategically choosing looser pants in advance, a buffer can provide the time needed between milestones, preventing your project from getting stuck in a bind. Plan for it, know it, and leverage it.

**Timelines Reveal Truth:** It's natural for members of new teams not to immediately trust one another. I recently took over an in-flight project with teams spanning four countries and wasn't sure of their habits or whether I could really trust them. I'm quite sure that feeling was mutual, as the prior leader has been dismissed under less-than-ideal circumstances. Stepping in just before a key delivery milestone, I asked a lot of questions—until I got comfortable we could achieve our milestone. There was friction, but through that process, I learned whom I could trust and learned to trust what my team was telling me. Many times, it took triangulation on both sides before we found our way to common understanding in pursuit of our common objective: project delivery.

**Just the Facts:** Bad news doesn't age well. Start signaling risks as they become realistic and material. But don't get emotional about risk. Look at facts and how those facts will impact the realistic budget, schedule, scope, and quality. When the impact will be material based on these facts, then escalate the risk and notify others.

The bottom line is that risk breeds uncertainty. Uncertainty causes anxiety and fear, freezing people in their boots. Sometimes we need to be rattled to move us past uncertainty into action.

## Planning for Plan B

Some cultures are extremely risk-averse, donning shiny suits of armor as they ready for battle. Others embrace risk while valiantly beating their chests and howling at the sky. Understanding how your culture deals with risks will help you position your Plan B.

For those cultures who armor up to account for every risk, know that most of your project overhead will be spent in planning, reporting, and ensuring risks never materialize. When they do, process takes over, and you must execute risk remediation while assuring upper management that all will be well.

It can be exhausting spending hours of each day managing communications among all the stakeholders. You quickly learn not to take risks and to slow-roll projects. You frame everything in "should" and "could" while deferring commitment until you are absolutely sure you can achieve the outcome you have signed for in blood. Fraught with anxiety, this culture requires you to learn the game, execute well, and build trust with stakeholders around the organization.

Conversely, cultures who frame risk as "failing faster" often burn hot with passion and creativity. Plan B isn't so much a plan as it is one of many dirt trails leading through the wilderness in pursuit of the largest game you can bag. Project managers in this culture will spend most of their time vacillating between wishing for better process and apologizing to customers and team members about yet another change in direction. Quality will be a perpetual concern, but the culture of fail faster always comes with creative bandages for the inevitable skinned knees and bloody faces.

I've worked in both cultures and many in between. I wondered for a long while whether there were any universal lessons to planning for the inevitable risk coming to pass. Aside from dealing with the emotional self-regulation discussed previously, there are two key hallmarks that will inform how you frame your Plan B.

**Roadmaps for the Win:** I've worked in the technology sector for most of my career. Companies proffer roadmaps summarizing vision and product direction. In other industries, leaders showcase goals and aspirations to "get everyone on board." After years of watching, preparing, and presenting corporate roadmaps myself, I now leverage these to gauge how adaptable and proactive the organization is. By aligning project plans to use similar framing, jargon, and visuals to these roadmaps and leadership messages, we can gain buy-in and accelerate moving past the risk to outcome with less drama.

**Discounts Are for Losers:** I once managed a team that missed a key update to customer software. This created a security gap the customer demanded be closed. The problem was going to take six months to fix, so we suggested the sales team offer a discounted version of the higher-tier software to help our customer out in the meantime. The CEO questioned why our failure required the company to sacrifice revenue. This view clearly prioritized us over our customer and the transaction over the relationship, telling me a lot about how my Plan B was to be managed in the future.

Diligently observing how organizations communicate their plans and deal with misses will show you a lot about how to frame your own Plan B. When should you plan meticulously? When should you fail fast and ask forgiveness later? Using these two reference points, all will become clear as you observe, implement, and interact with your stakeholders.

## Mission, Not Methods

I can't tell you the number of times I've gotten so focused on doing something the same way I've always done it that I looked right past obvious (and sometimes easier) answers to solve my immediate obstacles. Habits make slaves of us all.

The Air Group's officers had gotten so used to getting plans via email that they forgot about other ways to do the job. It took a scalding hot cup of reality—in the form of the colonel screaming at us all—to wake everyone up. Despite that moment being seared into my brain, I still find myself getting stuck sometimes.

What's the mission again?

Asking this question often keeps me focused and in pursuit of progress. I am mindful of when I'm becoming dogmatically focused on the way something has to get done rather than what my objective was in the first place.

Through years of military and martial arts training, I've learned the point of repetitive training is to engrain reflexive action without thought. Most adopt habits out of convenience, but we must do the hard work and train for adaptability and mental flexibility under the pressure of realized risks.

The officers adopted a habit of method without retaining focus on the mission. In our pursuit to become the unconscious competent, we must remain aware of our tendency to allow habit to blind us when the path we have become used to traveling closes to us.

If you think of risk as a math equation where the outcome is a known quantity, then the rest of the variables can be interchangeable. By allowing yourself the mental flexibility of swapping one set of variables for another, you can begin to see an increasing number of possible paths to navigate around and through the realized risk. More options provide greater opportunity to achieve the same, known outcome.

## Get Those Birds in the Air

Any way you slice it, dealing with risk is a dirty business. My advice is to do the best you can. Don't get emotionally strung out. You will always be judged by others for how you plan for, react to, and move through risks. Whether you successfully mitigate the risk or take a hit to scope, budget, schedule, or quality, it is all a reflection of your acumen. But that doesn't mean it's a reflection of your worth. Resilient project leaders will recognize the mistake, move to action, and manage through. It's true bad leaders and customers will skewer you and hang you out to dry. Take your lumps, learn from your mistakes, and get those birds in the air!

## Parting Embers

As you soar through the unpredictable skies of project management, remember this: Risk is inevitable, but your response to it defines your success. Here are the essential lessons for managing uncertainty and maintaining resilience:

- **Embrace Uncertainty:** Uncertainty is unknowable but manageable. Focus on what you can control, and proceed with confidence.
- **Plan for Plan B:** Always have a contingency plan. Whether your culture is risk-averse or risk-embracing, understanding how to adapt is crucial.
- **Prioritize the Mission:** Stay focused on the end goal, not just the methods. Flexibility and adaptability are your allies in achieving project success.
- **Communicate Risks Early:** Bad news doesn't age well. Signal risks as they arise, stick to the facts, and be proactive in your responses.

- **Avoid Getting Emotional:** Resilient project leaders must manage risk without getting emotionally strung out. Regardless of the outcome, it reflects on your acumen, not your worth.

Project management is not about avoiding risks but handling them with resilience and clarity. Your legacy in project management will be defined by how you navigate the storms and keep your mission on course. So keep those birds in the air, and remember, it's not just about the destination, but how you get there.

## SEVENTEEN

## Crisis Management: Duck, Cover, and What Comes Next

"Success is not final, failure is not fatal: It is the courage to continue that counts."

—Winston Churchill

I stood in one of many cement bunkers with a dozen other Marine recruits in South Carolina, watching Staff Sgt. Morris showing Stevens how to pull the pin, release the clip, and throw the M67 fragmentation grenade as hard as he could downrange. Stevens nodded sheepishly, fully aware of the gravity of the situation—perhaps too much so.

Staff Sgt. Morris handed Stevens the live grenade. "Prepare to throw!" Staff Sgt. Morris barked.

"Prepare to throw, aye, sir!" Stevens exclaimed, his voice cracking.

"Throw!" Staff Sgt. Morris yelled.

Stevens inserted his finger into the grenade's pin, preparing to pull as he'd been repeatedly instructed. He pulled the pin with his left hand. Whether due to sweaty palms, poor dexterity, or some combination, Stevens popped the grenade clear out of his right hand. It dropped on the ground between them with a dull thud, the clip popping off with a metallic ping. Both looked at the small, gray pineapple in shock. I couldn't look away!

Aghast, I watched from the bunker. Staff Sgt. Morris didn't hesitate: "Live grenade! Cover! Everyone, cover!"

Everyone dove for cover, most hiding in their bunkers while the rest swooped headfirst into fighting holes scattered across the sandy field. From our bunker, I watched on. In one smooth motion, Staff Sgt. Morris scooped up the live grenade and chucked it downrange. I ducked behind the concrete stoop of the bunker. Just after cresting the height of its arc, the grenade exploded in midair, sending shrapnel racing outward in all directions.

As I peeked over the bunker step to see if the two were still in one piece, a shard of twisted metal landed just in front of me, punctuating the scene with the finality of a period. My eyes shifted focus from the wisp of smoke rising off the Parris Island sand to Staff Sgt. Morris. There he stood. The air cleared, and people started mulling about.

Staff Sgt. Morris offered some stern corrections to Stevens and, to my shock, put another grenade in his hand.

"Prepare to throw!" Staff Sgt. Morris barked. This grenade was lobbed as far as Stevens' arm could throw it.

Off in the distance, we felt and heard the grenade explode: Boom!

Staff Sgt. Morris glanced back casually at my bunker: "Next!"

## When Crisis Strikes

The plan just went out the window. Forget about your plan for now. Focus on what's right in front of you.

When you're in the thick of a project crisis, remember the famous mantra from *Hitchhikers Guide to the Galaxy*: "Don't panic." Crises can often devolve when human emotion overpowers logic and process. What would've happened if Staff Sgt. Morris had panicked? Sadly, many tend to lose their cool, scramble around mindlessly doing random stuff, and rush to try to convict the guilty party out of some sense of premature justice. Staff Sgt. Morris did none of that. You see, panic is more contagious than COVID-19. Besides that, it's pointless. Remember, when you're the project leader, you're the captain of the ship—even when it feels like it's sinking.

Instead, try the following:

**Accept:** Easier said than done, right? Here's a little secret: Accept the reality of the situation here and now. The first step in any crisis is to recognize it is happening, accept it, and prepare to act.

**Assess:** This isn't the time for guesswork. What do we know? What do we need to know? Gather facts, not rumors or assumptions.

**Prioritize:** Not all problems are created equal. Tackle the fires that are burning the hottest first. If everything is a priority, nothing is.

**Assign:** Decide who is going to do what and assign them to the tasks. Set expectations. Give timelines.

**Decide, Adapt, Act:** Once you've got an actionable plan, act. Keep adjusting the plan as new information comes in.

**Communicate Clearly:** Tell your team what's going on. Keep stakeholders up to date. Don't sugarcoat things, but no doom and gloom, either. Just the facts. Remember, a confused team is a useless team.

## Red Is My Friend

Even better than managing through a crisis is avoiding it in the first place. The project team should always be on the lookout for problems early and often, identifying risks that could boil over. The project manager is then able to align people to the risk, enact mitigation plans, and communicate progress toward resolution. To avoid crisis, lean on the mantra "Red is my friend."

Many project management tools and reports use the color red to indicate problems, risks, or delays. The saying emphasizes the importance of transparency and early identification of issues within a project. Bad news doesn't keep, so it's best to call out problems early and assemble a plan to manage them.

**Spot Trouble Early:** If you see red flashing in your reports or on your dashboard, it's not time to hide under the desk. It means trouble's brewing, and you've got a chance to jump on it before it turns into an inferno. It's like seeing smoke coming from your engine and knowing you gotta deal with it before it blows up.

**No Secrets Here:** When it comes to projects, secrets are about as useful as a screen door on a submarine. Being upfront about the messes and muddles means everyone can stop playing the blame game and start fixing things. It builds trust, and let me tell you, trust is like gold in this business.

**Mistakes Are Gold Mines:** Found a problem? Good. That's not a sign you failed; it's a sign you're about to learn something priceless. Each blunder is a chance to get smarter, sharper, and ready to avoid the next pitfall. It's like finding out the stove is hot; next time, you won't touch it.

**Quit the Finger-Pointing:** Let's not worry about who landed the truck in the ditch. Let's just get it out and get back on the road. Fix issues together. Don't waste time deciding who's to blame in the moment. Sure, team members want to learn from mistakes to grow, but don't use fault as a weapon to bludgeon others with.

**Steer Clear of Icebergs:** Spotting the red flags early means you can change course before you hit an iceberg. It's about managing risks, not wearing blinders. Adjust your plans, shuffle your resources, and maybe, just maybe, you'll skirt disaster.

In the end, it's important to build a culture of acceptance of and learning from mistakes. Don't be scared to admit there are problems. Face them head-on, learn from them, and work together to fix them. During a crisis, being honest and preferring action over analysis enables teams to avoid crisis where possible and achieve victories when faced with calamity.

## Autopsying the Corpse of Crisis

At some point, the crisis is over. The team saved the day, everyone high-fives, and then the group is tasked with a root cause analysis. These lookbacks can be wonderful in helping an organization learn from a crisis and take steps to improve to avoid similar crises in the future.

But as helpful as postmortems can be, I rarely see root cause analyses result in any meaningful change.

Sometimes, if the situation is bad enough, leaders will resign or be dismissed. Over my years, I have been surprised to have seen almost no scapegoats offered up to appease the masses after a crisis. Instead, the great tragedy of organizational management is more insidious and far less glamorous. The first outcome is that the team knows the real problem yet dodges the truth of the matter, knowing the culture is too risk-averse to accept any material criticism. The second outcome is that the team makes tangible recommendations that are ultimately swept aside because changing things is harder than just playing the odds another crisis won't happen again.

I've found that pain is a wonderful motivator. It is acute enough to elicit reaction. It can be guided to achieve a particular outcome you may desire. But pain is temporal. After the crisis has abated, busy leaders often rush off to some new problem du jour. You lose their attention after the pain has passed. By solving the problem, you get the accolades of the moment, but the real solution fades in the wash. The opportunity of crisis is a window in time in which savvy project managers can exploit action by exposing but not rushing to relieve the pain.

Admittedly, this is a delicate balance that doesn't always go as planned. Hold out on solving the problem too long, and someone will be appointed to step in and solve the problem you couldn't (or wouldn't). Solve the problem too quickly, and you'll have successfully planted the seed that the team can manage this the same way in the future, affecting no real change.

Making the case for change, then, is of utmost importance in your findings and recommendations. The more severe the problem, the more likely that felt pain was shared by decision-makers. If not, you'll want to ensure you clearly make your case for change.

David Gleicher created a simple and elegant equation that addresses the reasons why changes succeed or fail, known as Gleicher's change equation:

---

$SD \times V \times FS < R = C$

---

If **S**hared **D**issatisfaction times **V**ision times **F**irst **S**teps is greater than **R**esistance, it will equal a successful **C**hange. However, if any of the factors on the left side of the less-than sign are zero, that entire side will turn to zero, with resistance taking over.

Leaders may often cover one or two of the initial three items but miss a third. For example, they tend to come up with a clear **V**ision or goals (V) and do a fine job of developing plans (FS), but they fail to make the case that change is needed (SD).

Review your root cause analysis to ensure you articulate each of the criteria and make the case for change clearly and concisely.

Managing crisis ain't about the adrenaline of putting out the fire. When the dust settles, and you're standing amidst the rubble of what was once a perfectly good plan, remember that it's about staying calm, moving through the crisis, and seizing the opportunity to help the organization (and its people) grow.

You know all this. The real challenge is whether others understand, too. Most will read the reports, nod sagely, and then it's back to business as usual. All those lessons learned are filed away to gather dust. Crisis management isn't for the faint of heart. It's for the steely-eyed, quick-thinking, tough-as-nails project manager who knows that when the fit hits the shan, it's an opportunity for growth. Recognition of need happens when confronted with pain. But growth requires deliberate commitment to applying corrections and continuing to execute the plan.

Next time you find yourself staring at a live grenade that just rolled between your feet, be decisive, seize the moment, and remember not to drop the grenade the second time. Next!

## Parting Embers

Crisis will strike in project management. When it does, remember that it's not your plan but your actions in the moment that determine the ultimate outcome. Being present, staying calm, and maintaining focus can turn disaster into a learning experience. Here are the key takeaways to navigate through crises effectively:

- **Accept and Assess Reality:** Recognize the

situation and gather factual information to understand what's happening.
- **Prioritize and Assign Tasks:** Tackle the most pressing issues first and clearly delegate responsibilities with set expectations.
- **Act and Adapt:** Implement your plan and be ready to adjust as new information comes in. Keep your team and stakeholders informed with clear, concise communication.
- **Embrace Transparency:** Use "red flags" as opportunities to address issues early and build trust within your team.
- **Learn From Mistakes:** Treat crises as learning opportunities. Conduct root cause analyses to identify and implement meaningful changes.
- **Seize the Moment:** Use crises as a chance to push for necessary changes and improvements within the organization.

Crises are not simply challenges; they are opportunities for growth. By accepting the reality, assessing the situation, prioritizing tasks, acting decisively, communicating clearly, and learning from mistakes, you can manage through any storm. When the dust settles, it's the lessons learned and the changes implemented that truly define your success.

## EIGHTEEN

## Falling Victim to Fads and Gimmicks

---

"What has been is what will be, and what has been done is what will be done; there is nothing new under the sun."

—Ecclesiastes 1:9 CSB

---

"We're moving to a new CRM!" Jimmy announced to his sales team, splaying his hands out as if measuring a fish he'd caught. "Tomorrow, we'll all get together in the conference room. Ken will help us load the software, and we'll go through a few hours of training. We'll have lunch together, and then y'all can get out there and make the most of it!"

I scanned the room, stopping briefly on each face to gauge reactions. This was our company's fourth CRM change in as many years. It wasn't like the sales team was doing a bad job; we'd grown revenues by 3X over that time.

After the meeting, I had a few moments with Jimmy, our VP of sales, and Bob, our president. "The sales team has been doing pretty well. What are you hoping for with this newest system, Jimmy?" I asked.

"Oh, it's got solid integration with our billing system so reps can get current numbers for our accounts. It also lets us control the reps' access to our records better so they can't take our customers with them."

"Is that a problem with our reps?" I inquired.

"Nah, but you never can be too safe," Jimmy explained. "Besides, our reps aren't really using the current system very well."

"What's different this time?" I asked with a slight inflection at the end of my question so as not to sound as cynical as I felt.

"Uh, it's a new system … " he trailed off as if the answer was self-obvious. "But the best thing is—get this—the screen looks like index cards!" Jimmy left that hanging in the air, expecting more of a reaction. Seeing his point wasn't landing, he continued. "It's just like how I used to manage my territory before all the fancy software was available. I figure a lot of our reps will really get a kick out of it!"

The next day, the reps gathered around the large round conference room table. The lights were dimmed, and their faces were aglow with the backlit computer screens.

"It's asking for 'server name.' What's the server's name, Ken?" Tony asked.

"Icarus dot company dot com, Tony," I responded.

"Oh, like that story about the kid who made himself wings to fly?" Tony asked.

"That's right, Tony. Exactly like that story. Do you remember how it ended?"

Tony's eyes searched the ceiling for the answer before he gave up with a shrug.

The room contentedly carried on. I shook my head and went back to work, dismayed that the ending of the story seemed lost on everyone. Next year, Jimmy rolled out Salesforce.

## Sticking to What Works

Jimmy was always chasing the new, shiny bauble. That behavior had served him well in his own career, after all. Why wouldn't he?

His team was performing well, but they could be even better. His team wasn't really using the software, either. "If they just used it the right way, they'd be more efficient and do even better," he thought.

Rather than dig in and learn the motivations behind poor adoption, he assumed changing the software would solve the problem. Jimmy never considered how his sales reps perceived the software. It was an obstacle in their day—drudgery. It wasn't seen as a tool enabling them to be more efficient. Jimmy never considered that his own need for control over his reps' activities influenced his choices. He played victim to an unseen puppet master year after year.

Flashy may be well-suited for commercials and action flicks, but in my observation, flashy isn't usually the best for project management. What works are tried and true methods that have stood the test of time—and for good reason. Whether you're talking about CRM software or project management, the common denominator is human behavior. So long as we have humans involved in projects, you'll need clear goals, solid planning, realistic timelines, effective communication, and a solid understanding of stakeholder motivations.

**Get Clear Goals:** You've got to know where you're going. A project without clear goals is a ship without a rudder; you'll just float around aimlessly. Set your objectives straight and make sure everyone knows what they are.

**Create Solid Planning:** I can't stress this enough. Plan your work, then work your plan. You can have all the fancy tools in the world, but if you haven't laid out a good plan, you're building on sand.

**Expect Iteration:** Often, customers and executives deliver generalized desires they like to call goals or outcomes. You're expected to understand and work with the team to craft the plan on how to make it happen. Rare is the case in which a goal stands the test of scrutiny. It is often the case that the scrutiny of planning creates more questions. Thus, the plan can often help to refine and clarify the goals. Regardless of your management frameworks, expect and embrace this back-and-forth.

**Set Realistic Timelines:** Set timelines that make sense. I've seen too many projects crash and burn because a team didn't think about timelines and delivery. Timebox as much as you can as often as you can. Work toward goals in time. Understand when time can be an ally or enemy.

**Communicate Effectively:** Talk to your team. Raise risks early. Keep everyone up to speed with the project at the pace they need. Learn when to be proactive and when to let something sit. One size does not fit all. Miscommunication sinks more projects than anything else.

**Be Aware of Stakeholder Motivations:** I've been burned several times for not taking time to understand someone's motivation. Understanding motivations doesn't have to be a soap opera drama. It just takes empathy and understanding that others have their own stuff going on. Understand how to help them win by helping you. Build relationships early and often.

## Pursue Moderation in All Things

Humans are insatiable, and our constant desire for new experiences is well-documented. This thirst for something new—be it driven by evolutionary impulses, learned behaviors, or a melding of the two—propels us into a world that caters to our craving for the bigger, better, and unprecedented. It is in our very nature to remain perpetually unsatisfied; this drive has led to our greatest breakthroughs and inventions. Yet, if left unchecked, it can lead us to ruin. If we reflect, we can recall many great catastrophes caused by the unchecked pursuit of ambitions.

Sure, you can experiment with new trends, but you gotta know what works. To effectively navigate these waters, you must anchor yourself to the above principles. Remember, the most important tool in your toolbox isn't a methodology or software; it's your common sense. if something doesn't feel right, it likely isn't. Don't get blinded by the shiny packaging.

Chasing the new for its own sake is foolish. Yet we can't be complacent, never challenging the status quo. Experiment frequently. Commit cautiously. Align outcomes to motivations. Balance innovation with wisdom. Pursue moderation in all things. This is how you avoid falling victim to fads and gimmicks.

## Parting Embers

I get excited about shiny, new things, too! However, chasing every new trend can be as detrimental as refusing to innovate at all. The allure of the latest trends and innovations can be incredibly tempting. While it's thrilling to explore new possibilities, it's crucial to stay anchored in tried-and-true principles. Here are some things to think about:

- **Get to the Root:** Focus on understanding and resolving underlying issues rather than relying on flashy new solutions.
- **Stick to the Basics:** Clear goals, solid planning, realistic timelines, effective communication, and an understanding of stakeholder motivations are essential for success.
- **Balance in Everything:** Pursue new trends with caution, anchoring decisions in common sense and proven methods to avoid falling for fads and gimmicks.

Moderation is your compass. It will guide you through the temptations of fads and gimmicks, ensuring you deliver consistent and reliable results. When you feel dazzled by the shiny packaging, take a step back and reassess. Is this innovation aligned with your core principles? A balanced approach will help you avoid falling victim to fleeting trends and ensure you achieve lasting success.

## NINETEEN

## Embrace the Suck

---

"The impediment to action advances action. What stands in the way becomes the way."

—Marcus Aurelius

---

Marine Corps 2nd Recruit Training Battalion stood just outside the barracks at dusk. Loaded for bear, we stood in formation with our 60-pound rucksacks and M-16s slung over our shoulders. The Crucible was a 54-hour-long circuit test—the culmination of 70 days of training leading to this point.

Were we prepared?

With the sun now set, we readied ourselves for the inevitable start of our journey. "Forward march!" the drill instructor called, emphasizing each syllable with a synchronized jut of his jaw. We looked ahead in the dim light of Parris Island, attempting to discern our chances with only a patchwork of hints of what to expect.

Over the duration, our physical, mental, and emotional reserves were taxed beyond our expectations. We rationed 1 1/2 meals over 2 1/2 days. I discovered I could compensate by drinking as much Gatorade as possible to get as many calories as I could while staying hydrated. We found time between exercises to nod off for 15 minutes, hoping to compensate for the meager 2 1/2 hours of sleep each night. It was all a struggle.

Drill instructors rained down coarse insults and instructions interchangeably as we belly-crawled through sandy, wet mud. Every so often, one of us got a boot to the back of our helmet, forcing us to taste the thick, brackish sludge. After crawling for what felt like hours, we were commanded to get to our feet and form up. Our green cammies now brown with mud, we double-timed it to our next obstacle while trapped water sloshed out of the tops of our waterlogged boots.

We moved on to the day movement course as our energy flagged. Then came the combat course and the night movement course—a relentless cadence of tests aimed to test our mettle. Moments of rest were few and far between, acutely stripping away all vanities. Tempers flared regularly. Finally, the last obstacle remained: our 9-mile hike back to base, where we would achieve our hard-fought designation of United States Marine.

Running low on food and sleep, we had to find a new type of fuel. We had to embrace the suck and dig deep within ourselves to achieve our goal. Exhausted, we sang to keep our minds engaged and spirits lifted. Around mile 7, I felt light-headed. I wanted to finish, but I was close to passing out. To have come so far and fall out was unthinkable. I started to trail the group, and a medic slipped me a PowerGel pack. I shakily tore it open and squeezed the contents into my mouth. Strength returned as the calories and electrolytes hit my bloodstream. I could finish.

I stood on the parade deck of Parris Island with the early morning splashing all around. A drill instructor walked up to me, turned, and placed the Eagle, Globe, and Anchor in my hand. Tears welled up as I realized I had achieved something I never imagined possible just a few months prior.

As Marines, we learned to lean into adversity because it builds resilience of the body, mind, and character. There were many times I wanted to give up. It was too hard without food. It was too hard without sleep. It was all too hard. But each time I faced that feeling, I let it wash over me and embraced the suck. I screamed to muster the energy I needed to get over a wall. I blew bubbles when my head got shoved in a mud puddle. I let myself feel the present moment and embrace how bad it all felt, allowing the adversity to illuminate and fuel my next step.

## Adopt a Salty Sense of Survival

A salty attitude is a perspective developed by people who've been around the block, seen some stuff, and aren't afraid to tell it like it is—even if it stings a bit. Developing this salty attitude isn't a luxury; it's a survival skill. It's the distance you need to see the punch coming. It's the armor you wear when you're about to face the monster. It's what keeps you frosty while the noobs chase the next project management framework du jour.

There's a kind of joy in this salty perspective. It's the kind of joy you get from knowing that no matter how messy things get, you've been through worse and survived. When you've been in the trenches as long as I have, you learn to appreciate the small moments. You start to find joy in the little things: a meeting that actually helps the team make progress, a timeline that doesn't blow up, or a team member who actually does what they're supposed to without needing their hand held every step of the way.

Being salty also means you avoid falling victim to the traps others set for you. Early in my career, I'd often be walking along, minding my own business, and suddenly realize I'd fallen into a dark pit. Initially, I had no idea how to get out; the walls were too high. With a little more experience, I now recognize most of these traps well before they ensnare me. I refuse to let others bait me into sharing their stress and fear-riddled urgency. Free from these emotional ambushes, I keep my priorities in focus. I then take stock of how I might serve up a solution while avoiding getting pulled into all the drama.

Try to dodge the traps whenever you can. The real secret is to be grateful for every moment, no matter how challenging. And when you find yourself facedown in the mud, make the most of it; blow some bubbles!

## Secrets to Being Salty

If you're a new or frustrated project manager, how do you achieve this salty outlook—especially if you don't have three decades of trial and error like me? Here's the ladder I suggest you climb:

**Get Straight on Your 'Why':** When faced with screaming managers, crying customers, and a relentless barrage of challenges, I turn inward. Deep in my heart, where my faith resides, I find love for all like my God loves me. This centers me, reminding me of the blessings of my family. Everything else falls into the category of "wants." During crises, keeping this true purpose vividly in my mind's eye enables me to navigate the turmoil effectively. Before adversity strikes, take time to clearly understand and emotionally connect with your own purpose.

**Be Honest With Yourself:** Many have a tendency to disengage from challenging situations. I find many twist or omit facts to soften a perceived impact or backlash. This is dangerous thinking that is corrosive to teams and totally acidic to one's character, diminishing the ability to execute effectively. At all times, face the truth and be honest with yourself about it. This is crucial to living, to survival. I find it no less impactful during less critical work, even if only to keep the knife's edge sharp.

**Always Be Curious:** Don't rush in assuming you know everything. Don't assume you know everyone's agendas. Instead, always stay curious. Lean in, ask questions, and seek understanding. This is a key skill to develop so you can avoid being pulled into the emotional traps hungry for scrambling victims who don't know their way out.

**Stay Calm When Trapped:** When faced with the runaway emotions of being triggered, learn to recognize your own circumstances are a construct. Where choices appear limited, acknowledge your own emotions, accept them, then align. Once aligned, you can more clearly reevaluate options and take steady steps to find freedom and attain your goal.

**Remember the Discomfort Razor:** This is a principle that suggests, when faced with multiple options, the one that challenges us more significantly should be considered more seriously or chosen over more comfortable options. Facing adversity often leads to growth, while electing to follow a comfortable path tends to lead to stagnation.

**Carpe Diem:** Seize the day! Gratitude is an important practice in staying salty. While most associate a salty attitude with cynicism, it doesn't mean you should focus solely on the unpleasantness of your situation.

Sure, you may want to toss your smoldering cigar butt on the gasoline-doused floor to burn the whole place down sometimes. But this shouldn't be your primary mode of operation. Once you've experienced some tough times, it becomes a bit clearer you should savor the small moments life offers. Until then, live this mantra to ensure you stay sane and keep a resilient perspective.

## Parting Embers

Perseverance is forged in the fires of adversity. Resilience isn't built by avoiding challenges but by facing them head-on. Here are the key takeaways to help you embrace the suck and emerge stronger:

- **Face Adversity Head-On:** Challenges are inevitable. Lean into them and let each struggle build your resilience. The more you embrace the tough times, the more prepared you'll be for the next obstacle.
- **Stay Focused on Your "Why":** In the chaos of demanding projects and high-stress situations, your purpose is your anchor. Reconnect with your core values to navigate through the toughest storms.
- **Cultivate a Salty Attitude:** Experience teaches you to see traps before they catch you. Use your hard-earned wisdom to stay grounded, keep your priorities straight, and avoid getting sucked into unnecessary drama.

We've journeyed together through the arduous path of embracing adversity, pushing beyond the limits of our endurance, and discovering the raw power of resilience. The narrative of our trials—exemplified in my own journey through the grueling Crucible and the moment I received the Eagle, Globe, and Anchor—serves as a testament to the indomitable spirit within each of us. Let us carry forward the lessons learned in the mud and under the weight of challenge. Remember, when faced with the inevitable trials that life throws our way, the strength to overcome doesn't emerge from avoiding the struggle but from the courage to embrace it. So as you move forward, take a deep breath, set your sights on your goal, and embrace the suck.

TWENTY

## Escape Your Job's Emotional Shackles

---

"The price of anything is the amount of life you exchange for it."

—Henry David Thoreau

---

"We've got to have this statement of work over to the bank tomorrow!" Mike exhaled, exasperated, as he plopped down in the chair opposite my desk.

I looked up from my computer screen. "Mike, it's December 23rd."

"I know, but Ethan—you know Ethan, our buyer, right?" Mike began to search my face, seeming to attempt to gauge my comprehension, but carried on despite any confirmation. "Ethan needs this in his inbox to review for a Monday meeting with the CFO for approval."

"Is the bank even open Christmas Eve?"

Mike whipped out his phone and dialed Ethan for an impromptu conference call. "Hey, Ethan, it's Mike. I've got you on speaker with Ken."

"Hey, guys," came Ethan's nasally tenor over the mobile phone's speaker. "Ken, we need this proposal from you to keep the train on the tracks. You gotta help us out here."

Over the course of the next ten minutes, the duo tag-teamed me like an overly dramatized WWE title match of the late '80s. They made it abundantly clear that everything hinged on this statement of work to green-light the project. There was no time to waste.

"So, you got this?" Mike asked, seeking confirmation as he stood up to leave. He lobbed a trailing grenade as both question and exclamation: "If we can sink this shot, you know how many doors it will open?"

I opened the draft document and began my work. At 7 in the evening, my wife called and asked if I was planning to come home anytime soon. Feeling guilt and shame at missing dinner, I packed up and left.

The next day—Christmas Eve—our office was working a half-day. As lunchtime came, I wished my team a Merry Christmas and happy holidays, then returned to the task at hand. I still had a lot left to do.

By midafternoon, stragglers noticed me and came by to wish me well as I toiled away at the delicate proposal.

Afternoon turned into evening as the click-clacks of my keyboard provided the only soundtrack in the empty office. Every so often, I'd push back from the desk and meander through the rows of cubicles, dimly lit by the few fluorescent bulbs still on. The open floor plan was eerily empty, with only occasional holiday decorations reminding me it was Christmas Eve. After my rounds, I returned to my chair to carry on with my important work.

I didn't want to be there. "It'll make a difference," I thought, attempting to convince myself the mission mattered more than time with my family.

As the clock hands rolled through 5, 6, and then 7, I ached to be done. Just before 8, I finally finished my work. I prepared my email, ensured I attached the document, reread the email one last time, and pressed send. I knew I'd receive warm thanks for coming through on this tight deadline.

Christmas came and went, and we returned to the office Monday. Nothing from Ethan. As midmorning came to a close, I wondered about the outcome of the meeting. Monday passed, then Tuesday and Wednesday. I reached out to Mike to inquire about what was going on.

"Oh, Ethan's going in a different direction," was all he had to say.

## Recognize Your Prison

I learned a valuable lesson that Christmas: I was a hopeless, emotional prisoner to my job, enslaved to my own subconscious wounds and seeking validation through my work. I wasn't bonded by love of money or power; I was a prisoner of my own personal need for approval and praise.

Are you emotionally shackled to your job? How do you even know?

Perhaps you possess perfectionist traits and feel compelled to meticulously plan every detail before quitting, convinced that no one else can meet your high standards. You might exhibit people-pleasing tendencies, struggling to say no and sacrificing personal time and relationships out of a sense of obligation and duty. Or perhaps you find yourself entangled in office politics and drama, which, despite your claims of disdain, you secretly relish.

There are telltale signs. What follows is a checklist of the more common behaviors. The larger the number of these symptoms that resonate with you, the more likely you are to be an emotional prisoner:

**First In, Last Out:** You're always the first one to turn on the lights and the last one to leave. Home? What home? Your real address is your office chair.

**Working Lunches:** Your lunch breaks are an opportunity to catch up. You sit at your desk scarfing a sandwich or salad, calling it a "working lunch" as if that's some badge of honor.

**Vacation Accumulator:** You've got more unused vacation days than a squirrel has nuts for the winter. You might opine for time away at a tropical beach or secluded, mountain cabin, but you wind up hoarding vacation days like a miser because you're just too busy to take the time.

**Weekend Warrior:** Weekends are just two extra days for catching up on work, not for resting or, heaven forbid, having fun. Just a quick check in on Saturday morning or getting a head start on Sunday evening feels easier than letting it all go.

**Emotional Barometer:** Your mood swings with your successes and failures at work. A good day at the office means joy, and a bad day means everyone had better steer clear.

**Perpetual Pleaser:** You're constantly saying yes to every request, regardless of the cost to your own sanity. Your favorite word: "Sure!" (even though your eyes scream "Help me!").

**Overpreparation:** You like to prepare for simple presentations as if you're defending a doctoral thesis—charts, graphs, and a backup plan to the backup plan.

**Procrastination Paradox:** Sometimes you put off tasks because of fears it can't be done perfectly. The irony is that you're delaying because you care too much about getting it just right.

**Detail-Obsessed:** You'll focus on the tiniest details that no one else notices or cares about—like worrying about whether to use past, present, or future tense in your risk descriptions or obsessing over the font in your executive presentation.

**Can't Delegate:** You don't trust anyone else to meet the standard, so you wind up drowning yourself in work backlog. Delegation is like kryptonite to you; you'd rather do everything yourself and risk the meltdown. Besides, meltdowns are for true heroes anyway, right?

**Never Satisfied:** Your work is never done, never good enough. You're your own worst critic, always finding flaws where there aren't any.

**Feedback Fearer:** You take criticism harder than a hammer to your thumb. Even constructive feedback feels like a personal attack. You weather the feedback with a grimace but secretly beat yourself up for days to come.

**Constant Chatterbox:** You're always buzzing about the latest gossip. You claim to hate the drama but somehow are always the first to spill the beans.

**Information Hoarder:** You gobble up information and hold onto it like gold. While knowing the relevant scuttlebutt can offer a certain advantage, being emotionally pulled to know everybody's business is a sign you may be emotionally compromised.

**The Martyr:** You complain about being dragged into

the office politics yet somehow always find yourself in the thick of it, suffering for the cause.

Those who exhibit many of these behaviors are prime candidates for becoming emotionally overinvested in work because their self-worth is twisted up in their profession like a pretzel. If this sounds like you—even a little bit—what can you do about it?

## Free Your Mind

Thankfully, all hope is not lost. Over the span of my adult life, I've realized there are deliberate patterns I can follow and actions I can take to break the chains of my own emotional bondage.

You see, work is specifically designed as a meritocracy. The economic contract between work and worker is the exchange of wages for work performed. There is value and utility in this. However, so many of us define our sense of self-worth by our accomplishments. Ouch! That hurts to say out loud.

In all fairness, it's an overly tempting trap when we are lavished with gold stars, patted on our heads, and offered fancy-sounding titles in reward for our seemingly noble sacrifices. I fell into many such traps time and again because there are so many shades and variations that distract you until you recognize you're seeking to satisfy your own emotional needs in the process. I jumped from one role to the next—always climbing, always searching for the next mountain to summit. And I can promise you that if you give your all, work tirelessly, and brand your arm with the company logo, more doors of opportunity will open for you.

So what's the problem?

On the surface, this meritocracy appears to be a plausible and well-designed system. However, beneath its well-intended design, many individuals—including myself, and perhaps you, too—harbor an innate desire to attach more than monetary value to our achievements. It isn't wrong to be proud of work achievements, but linking personal worth to professional accomplishments creates an unstable foundation. In doing so, I conflated my personal needs with the design of the economic contract.

My employer paid me to perform a job. When I gave more than was asked, of course my employer was glad to accept my gifts. I was rewarded with plaques, promotions, raises, bonuses, trips, and trust. So long as I performed, I was rewarded. But I had built a prison from which I could not escape. American corporations and culture played their part, but I held the smoking gun.

If you wrestle with these issues, you can make the choice to do the hard work of separating your emotional dependency on achievements from defining your self-worth. In the epic words of Morpheus from *The Matrix*, "Free your mind."

## Break Your Emotional Chains

What practical steps can you take? Allow me to share the tools of my escape from emotional captivity.

**Know What You Are About:** Quit seeking approval; invest in yourself; and learn what nourishes your body, mind, and spirit. After years of counseling, decades of spiritual practice, and countless self-help books, I found my inner path. Once I found my footing, I felt less encumbered and met my day with more engagement and interest. People took notice that I was no longer seeking their approval. I was genuine and humble, and I found that my bosses respected me even more. As a fair warning, this will be a lifelong journey, and it is without the promise of accomplishment or ending. Still, Robert Frost's words resonate with my experience: "I took the one [road] less traveled by, and that has made all the difference."

**Set and Maintain Clear Boundaries:** Embrace the power of saying no and define the limits that protect and prioritize your well-being. Through personal reflection, prioritization, and consistent practice, I established my own limits. Once I committed to these boundaries, I discovered a newfound sense of freedom and control over my life. Others noted my assertiveness and respected my choices. As a result, I became more composed and decisive, which led my colleagues to trust and rely on me more deeply. Let this serve as a gentle reminder: Establishing firm boundaries is an ongoing process that requires diligence and courage.

**Say What You'll Do and Do What You Say:** Commit to the integrity of your word and fulfill your promises. Through clear communication and consistent actions, I cultivated a reputation for reliability. Repeated practice of this tenet reinforces balance in both my personal and professional life. Colleagues and friends alike began to trust in my dependability in turn, strengthening our relationships. The journey to becoming a person of your word is filled with continuous effort to deliver on your commitments.

**Communicate for Connection:** Prioritize understanding and empathy in every interaction to deepen your relationships. Through active listening and heartfelt expressions, I learned to truly engage with others' perspectives and emotions. This approach transformed simple exchanges into meaningful dialogues, fostering deeper connections with those around me. Colleagues, friends, and even strangers felt valued and heard, enhancing mutual respect and trust. Embrace this practice, as communication is not merely about conveying information but about building bridges between hearts and minds.

**Educate Others on How to Win With You:** Clearly articulate your expectations and the paths to success within your collaborations. By transparently sharing what drives my satisfaction and striving to understand others equally, I enable us all to learn how to win together. This openness not only clarifies our mutual objectives but also empowers those around me to contribute effectively and positively. As we engage in this shared journey, we build a foundation of mutual respect and understanding that elevates our collective achievements.

**Get a Hobby:** Cultivate activities that spark joy and enrich your life beyond your daily grind. By embracing pursuits that ignite my curiosity and passion, I've discovered levels of creativity and personal growth. Whether it's writing, martial arts, or hiking, engaging in my hobbies transforms idle hours into moments of joy and fulfillment. Your own personal pursuits offer a necessary escape from the mechanized gears of work and will enhance overall well-being by providing a fresh perspective about the world around us. Getting a hobby gives you a reason to leave work on time and serves as an escape hatch when the day's pressures mount.

Remember, work has no allegiance to you; it values you only to the extent that you serve its interests. When you cease to provide utility—in the form of your J-O-B—your fancy title and busy calendar will offer little comfort as you carry out your banker's box filled with desk knickknacks and that Employee of the Quarter certificate. It's crucial to recognize that in the end, it's just business. Free yourself from the emotional shackles that bind your self-worth to your work. Build a life rich with personal meaning and connections that persist beyond the confines of your job.

## Parting Embers

Your worth is not measured by your job title or achievements. Break free from the emotional shackles of work and find balance. Here are some things to remember:

- **Recognize Your Prison:** Just like the time I spent Christmas Eve in an empty office, driven by an unyielding need for validation, understand the signs that you are emotionally tied to your job, such as working excessively long hours and sacrificing personal time.
- **Set Clear Boundaries:** Learn to say no and define limits that protect your well-being. For instance, I committed to leaving the office by 6 p.m. daily, reclaiming my evenings for family and personal pursuits. I chose more enjoyable pursuits (such as a hobby) that didn't allow for staying late in the office. Combined, this led to increased respect and trust from others and more self-satisfaction.
- **Communicate for Connection:** Prioritize understanding and empathy in interactions to build deeper, more meaningful relationships. Opening dialogue with my team improved our working relationships and created a supportive environment. We learned how to help one another win.

Work will never value you beyond what you can offer it. By setting boundaries, fostering genuine connections, and seeking personal fulfillment outside the office, you can build a life that is rich and satisfying, both personally and professionally. Free your mind, live authentically, and thrive beyond the confines of your job.

## Finale | A Feast for the Vultures

"Your fat king and your lean beggar is but variable service—two dishes, but to one table. That's the end."

—William Shakespeare

At the start of it all, I told you to take what you want and leave the rest for the vultures. Did you learn anything in our time together?

You and I have slogged through the muck and mire of project management, page by page. From the highs of building your brand to the lows of choking on your own micromanagement, we've seen the beauty in breakdowns and the triumph in trusting the process. We've tasted the bitter truth about project management, debunked myths of perfect plans, and grappled with the art of expecting the unexpected.

Forget the sugarcoating. You're not here to be everyone's friend. You're here to get the job done. That means making tough decisions, having uncomfortable conversations, and often—more often, really—playing the bad guy. If you're looking for applause and pats on the back, you're in the wrong profession.

Mastering high-friction projects isn't about being a curmudgeon who hates change. It's about being realistic, pragmatic, and tough as nails. In the trenches of project management, the only thing you can truly count on is uncertainty. And if you can't stomach that, I suggest you consider a new line of work.

My hope is that this salty guide has provided a feast for your spirit as much as your mind. I hope you've gotten fat off a morsel or two of wisdom and a whiff of reality. As you loosen your belt, push back from the table, and allow your meal to digest, recognize the cupboard full of tactics to help you level up and excel well beyond your current station—for the remainder of your lifetime … or until you get to be as old as me, anyway.

As we part ways, let me leave you with this: In the end, you and I are just a feast for those feathered beasts. Remember that each day you clock in. Remember that when you feel your blood pressure rise after receiving another email from Jim in accounting. Remember that as you sit at your desk daydreaming of your slow-motion walk-away from the burning rubble of your project that just exploded in the background of your life's movie.

## Burn That Project Down

It's tempting to think the bridges you build or burn or the deadlines you meet or miss will be your legacy. But no; it's the choices you make that touch the people you meet along your journey. That is how you'll be remembered in the end.

Projects will come and go, as will the seasons of your career and life. In the end, no one has you handcuffed to your desk. To stay or go has always been your choice. So don't play the victim. Instead, remain steadfastly resolved to live out your own purpose.

What choice will you make? It's your move, and I hope you make it confidently—and with a dash of salt.

## About the Author

Ken Stewart's mission is to simplify choices and amplify focus for those navigating the bustling demands of life. Rooted in a deep-seated purpose to aid individuals and organizations in realizing their dreams, Ken's engagements have spanned from elevating personal productivity for teleworkers to launching award-winning programs for local enterprises and providing strategic insights for Fortune 500 giants.

A seasoned change management and delivery leader, Ken's three-decade career began in the U.S. Marine Corps and has spanned many roles in information technology and software development industries. His expertise includes strategic leadership, change and project management, and product development.

Ken is also passionate about the ministry of writing, which has been a source of hope and blessing in his life. Informed by years of hands-on experience and a deep understanding of the dynamics of change and project management, he champions team dynamics in support of organizational outcomes. More of Ken's writing can be found at ChangeForge.com, covering topics like artificial intelligence (AI), leadership, change and project management, and strategic alignment.

In his personal life, Ken draws inspiration from his beloved family. Melissa, his steadfast partner, has been a pillar of support through life's challenges. Outside of his professional life, Ken is an avid martial artist with nearly two decades of training in Beckham Hoshiki Aikido, Nihon Goshin Aikido, Yoshinkan Aikido, Yoseikan Aikido, and more recently in Moy Yat Ving Tsun.

www.ingramcontent.com/pod-product-compliance
Lightning Source LLC
Chambersburg PA
CBHW060318050426
42449CB00011B/2538